HUNTING FARMLAND BUCKS

John Trout, Jr.

How to hunt
North America's most popular
big game animal with bow and gun

Wild Trails Publishing

Trout, Jr. John 1946 ---
Hunting Farmland Bucks

Second Printing 1999

ISBN 0-9636526-0-5

Copyright © 1993 by John Trout, Jr.

Text and Photos by John Trout, Jr.

Illustrations Copyright © 1993 by Larry Smail

Wild Trails Publishing

Dedicated to the Ebenezer gang,
who I have shared hunting experiences
for more than 30 years.

ABOUT THE AUTHOR

John Trout, Jr. was born and raised in southern Indiana. He has spent more than 30 years pursuing the white-tailed deer at home and in several other areas of North America. An avid bow and gun hunter, specializing in deer, black bear, wild turkey and small game eventually led John to a full-time freelance career in outdoor writing and photography. He contributes regularly to several national and regional magazines, and authored his first book, *Trailing Whitetails*, in 1987.

ACKNOWLEDGMENTS

After three decades of deer hunting, I have realized that companionship in the field has contributed to the thousands of enjoyable hours I have spent pursuing whitetails. I owe special thanks to dad, and to my son John for spending many of those hours along side. Also, thanks to Eddie, Alva, Woody, Geary, Mark, Ross and Kevin for their fellowship in the deer hunting woods for countless years, and posing for photographs when there was always something better to do.

I thank my daughters, Alisa, Tammy and Kathy who have backed my hunting and writing over the years.

Thanks to Larry Smail for the fine artwork, and Jimmy Meyer, Steve Campbell, Joe Amiano and son Vito for assisting me when I needed photographs.

I appreciate the statistics and comments from several game and fish departments of those states and provinces that replied to my request.

I also want to thank Harris Publications, Bowhunting World, Bow & Arrow Hunting, Bowhunter, Petersen's Hunting, Game & Fish, Deer & Deer Hunting and other publications who previously published portions of a few chapters in this book. I would like to thank the Pennsylvania Game Commission for allowing me to write about their research, Professor Larry Marchinton and Karl Miller of the University of Georgia for their research data and comments, and Larry W. Richardson who several years ago provided research information surrounding deer communication.

A special thanks to my wife Vikki for providing support and understanding while I was in the field or sitting at the desk in front of the PC. I also owe her a great deal of gratitude for assistance in proofing and editing the pages that follow.

CONTENTS

INTRODUCTION

When I began deer hunting 30 years ago, the white-tailed deer had not yet flourished in Indiana. Although the stocking program started in 1934, the restoration success appeared to begin slowly in the farmland regions. Bag limits in 1961 allowed a hunter to take one antlered buck with either bow or gun, and hunters shared the season regardless of the weapon they chose. Other states practiced similar regulations while waiting for their deer herds to take hold.

The hunter now has the opportunity to fill several tags in about any state, particularly if they are a two-season hunter. And many farmland states that allowed only a few days of hunting opportunity 25 years ago, now offer several months to pursue whitetails.

Such developments as depredation and problem deer permits have become a common method to keep the deer herd from growing beyond our control. Perhaps the best word to use is necessary. Game and fish departments in most farmland states receive complaints from insurance companies about deer/vehicle collisions on a regular basis. Many state deer herds have more than doubled in the last decade, and it has become an obligation for them to reduce the herds.

We have learned how the white-tailed deer has adjusted to farmland regions, and continued to expand despite the efforts to control them. The proof is in this book, every hunting publication, and anyone who has spent time hunting them.

Many non-hunters do not realize the challenge of deer hunting in areas where a large percentage of the land is open country. They tend to believe that there is no place for the deer to hide, and that persistent hunting pressure will surely end in a hunter success situation. On the contrary, you and I know that any whitetail, and particularly the mature bucks, can escape whenever necessary to survive. They can disappear, regardless of the percentage of land that is agricultural. In this book you will discover how agricultural and woodlot mixtures vary in different states and provinces. While some may have higher percentages of farmland than others, the hunting changes very little. Hunters still pursue the food sources, escapes, and the rut no matter where it takes place. The techniques, however, will change accordingly.

This book is not about hunting trophy bucks. Instead, it focuses on all antlered whitetails. Although I have taken several good bucks with bow and gun, my main interest has leaned toward hunting all bucks. And like many hunters, I am fortunate to live in an area where trophies can be found, yet the bulk of the harvests consists of 1 1/2-year-old bucks. Although the techniques mentioned will slant toward hunting all bucks, there is no doubt they will help your trophy hunting, too. I also should mention that I am not against the harvesting of does. If deer are to be managed properly, the does must be regulated.

In recent years we have all contributed to putting bucks on a pedestal, or so it seems. Seldom do you see a publication publish an article about hunting just any whitetail. It seems we have been programed to think ''antlers'' any time we are in the field. Perhaps this, along with the feeling of more satisfaction, has reflected on my deer hunting. I can honestly say, though, that hunting bucks are different when compared to hunting just any whitetail. I do not condemn anyone for shooting a legal deer. It's just that there is an extra good feeling about slipping my tag on a deer that carries head-gear. I believe several deer hunters feel the same.

This book will provide you with both educational and how- to information at its fullest. If you hunt in any type of farmland country, and have an interest in pursuing bucks of any size, this book is sure to help. You will learn what time of year a certain technique should be used, and the reasoning behind it. Several biological researches also are mentioned to help you better understand how and why a buck reacts in various ways. This, along with the hunting techniques, should help you to become a more effective buck hunter in any farmland area.

We all have our own ideas on hunting bucks. That comes natural with experience and success. However, this book does not focus entirely on my opinions. You also will read testimonies from other successful and experienced individuals I have been fortunate enough to meet during recent years. Many of these hunters seem to specialize in one technique or another. Their advice has helped me on several occasions, and will be passed on to you.

Although it has been said before, I will say it again. The white-tailed deer is surviving and expanding in our own back-yards. They have learned to adjust to our way of life. For that reason they remain somewhat nocturnal. Perhaps that is also the reason why we pursue him with so much endeavor.

CHAPTER 1

PUBLIC VS. PRIVATE LAND

A century ago you could have hunted almost anywhere. It wasn't a matter of whether or not you were allowed to; only the amount of available game seemed to matter. Hunters and trappers shared these vast areas throughout North America, and seldom did interferences occur.

As time passed, certain game populations exploded, and so did the privilege to hunt in many areas. A great deal of government land was sold, and landowners began posting their ground at a rapid rate. The free-access lands quickly dwindled, forcing a growing number of hunters into smaller areas.

Hunting pressure plays a major role in the outcome of your hunt. I don't know any deer hunter who would deny that. Nor do I know of anyone who prefers to head for a crowded woods if another alternative is offered. Unfortunately, many agricultural areas that offer excellent hunting opportunities are privately owned. Public ground may exist in the heart of these same areas, but they are often over-crowded. I have enjoyed

11

success in both, but I will not say that public land offers equal opportunities. Hunting a private farm will usually increase your chances of success by a considerable margin. Whenever I can hunt an area that has fewer hunters and the quality habitat necessary for sustaining a deer herd, I usually jump at the chance. However, when it is not available I head for the public land like everyone else. And, I have learned methods that have helped me to be successful in the crowded areas. The bucks may have to be hunted differently, but they can be brought out by a persistent hunter who does a fair amount of homework. I have experienced several memorable, successful hunts in these areas, and I am sure I will have many more. But for some reason, things always appeared to look better on the other side of the fence. The thought of more solitude, along with the possibility of enjoying a successful hunt intrigues me. Simply said, private land is a major factor when hunting agricultural areas.

I sincerely believe that much of our hunting future depends on landowner/hunter relationships. The sportsmen must establish friendly relationships with landowners so that our future generations will have a place to hunt. But this is not an easy task. Some landowners have become anti's, while others remain non-hunters and do not give permission to anyone. A few of these who own large parcels of land, though, have joined forces with deer hunters and now allow hunting by permission.

There are basically three ways of gaining access to hunt on private land: gaining permission from a landowner, leasing the land for hunting rights, or simply sneaking in and taking your chances. Of course, we as hunters should consider only the first two choices as ethical. The courts look at trespassing as a crime, usually punishable by a small fine. However, some trespassers have found themselves on the wrong end of a gun. Landowners have taken it upon themselves to shoot and not ask questions. To most of us, trespassing may not warrant being shot, but it can and does happen. Fortunately, most landowners do not use these tactics. Most who post their ground make it clear that no one can hunt, or that permission must be given in advance, and for good reason.

I have seen several different types of signs posted by landowners in attempts to keep people from trespassing. I remember one that read, ''Enter at your own risk.'' I also recall an old logging road that was posted with a notice reading, ''Nails are waiting for your tires.''

Over the years I have asked many landowners for permission to hunt. This has included several out-of-state individuals, as well as people near my home. I have been

Private land may offer more opportunity when hunting pressure intensifies on nearby public land.

rejected more times than I care to mention, and I feel my odds are usually around 3 to 1 of obtaining permission. Naturally this depends on a given area. In some areas, everybody will let you hunt; in others no one grants permission. But I have noticed that landowners in most areas stick together when it comes to a decision. If one landowner doesn't allow you to hunt, there is a good chance the guy up the road will follow the same course. It seems that it becomes easier for them to pass out a rejection if everyone else does the same. Fortunately, this theory often works in reverse, favoring the hunter. When one individual gives permission, I make it a point to tell the next landowner in the same area, providing of course I am hoping to gain access to their land, too. They often give permission immediately when they know their neighbor gave the green light.

There have been some cases in which I worked on gaining permission from one individual, even though I didn't care all that much about hunting there. However, if that area connects to where I really wanted to go, I figured it could help when talking to the person who owned the best piece of ground. I always use an honest approach and explain that their ground offers the best hunting opportunity.

Before seeking permission, the hunter should be sure the private land will provide them with good hunting opportunities. There is no sense wasting time with an area if it does not appeal to you. And it does not necessarily mean that a trophy buck will walk into your lap just because you hunt on private land.

I will admit, though, that many heavily wooded public areas are bordered with agricultural fields that entice the deer. For this reason, I do most of my buck hunting close to the borders when hunting public areas. An excellent public area can easily be revealed when there is little or no cover on the nearby farms. The bucks will undoubtedly head for the denser public ground to bed, thus offering hunting opportunities.

When the surrounding private areas offer both food and cover, and the public ground provides the hunting pressure, you can be assured the bucks will head for the safety of the restricted farms.

Many farmland areas are endowed with roads. I spend time prior to opening day traveling these roads and glassing the agricultural fields. This often allows me to see how many bucks use a particular field, and gives me a good idea on the potential of a particular farm. I study the surrounding habitat as well, and then make a decision on hunting the area.

Topographic maps are vitally important. They will provide you with a detailed description of the area, and give you a good idea of the best access. You will always be better

Near dusk, this buck leaves the public area to feed in an agricultural field on private land.

prepared if you can explain your preferred access to the land-owner when you ask permission to hunt.

Plat maps are a necessity, simply because they will show you exactly how much property is owned, and who owns it. You can usually purchase them at a title office somewhere in the county you hunt. If they are not available, the title office can usually provide you with the information from their records, if you are prepared to tell them precise locations.

When asking permission, prepare yourself to hear all kinds of excuses when you get a negative answer. I remember one lady told me her son liked to play outside, and she feared a hunter might shoot him. She remained negative even when I explained that I would be hunting only during the archery season.

I even heard from one farmer that he wanted the deer to *take hold* better before he allowed anyone to hunt. I tried explaining that there are more than 150,000 whitetails in the state, and that "extra tags" had become common in the last decade to help control the herd, but his opinion did not change. He insisted on saying the area needed more deer.

Many hunters hear the oldest excuse in the book, and for good reason. These landowners quickly explain that their fences have been broken down and gates left open, allowing cattle to get out. This unfortunate reality will continue to plague responsible hunters for years to come. Regardless of how ethical some of us are, landowners judge us as a group. And when an unethical sportsmen gets on the bad side of a landowner, you can bet we will all suffer.

We must accept any reason when a landowner hands over a rejection. We always can promise the landowner that it will be different this time, but they always will have the right to decide if you will be allowed to hunt their property.

I don't feel, however, that a landowner should disrespect you just for asking. This unpleasant experience has happened to me on a few occasions. You plan the whole thing and ask very politely. Instead of hearing a friendly "No", you're ridiculed to the point of total fear, making it extremely difficult to ask anyone else. I believe if a hunter approaches a landowner in a courteous fashion, the landowner should respond in the same fashion, even if the answer is negative.

Several years ago I approached a farmer, asking for permission to continue trailing a wounded deer that I suspected had gone onto his property. I will not repeat the words he used, but I will say that I was ordered off his land immediately. He took a disrespectful attitude from the start, even though my approach was very polite. He simply hated all hunters, and nothing I could have said would have changed a thing.

Fortunately, few landowners take this kind of attitude when approached. Most will give you a polite answer when you use the same attitude, which is vitally important when hoping to receive a positive response.

I would not attempt knocking on a door, just because the dwelling is located in the vicinity you want to hunt. You would be surprised how many tenants live in the suburban and rural districts that own only a small lot. The plat map will provide you with names, and save you from asking permission from a farmer who owns only the crop fields. Many times I have asked permission to hunt, and discovered that my hunting area consisted of only a soybean or cornfield. The wooded areas surrounding the fields were often owned by someone else.

Always plan your approach. If needed, write down your lines and rehearse them before meeting with the individual. If you plan to call, read it off exactly the way you want it said. I've used this method many times, to ensure covering all bases.

HUNTING FARMLAND BUCKS

You should begin your friendly speech by telling him/ her your name and where you live. If you know anyone who knows them you also can offer a reference. This has helped me more than once. Tell the landowner why you want to hunt there,

Getting permission to hunt private land is often tricky business. A proper approach with the landowner is necessary.

the season dates and when you plan to be there. If it is necessary to scout in advance, then by all means let the person know. Some landowners don't understand the importance of pre-season scouting and may not understand you being there before the season begins.

A landowner often will refuse the opportunity to hunt because of too many people. Assure them in advance that you will not take Jim, Joe and Bob along unless agreeable with them. If you do wish to take an additional person, ask at the beginning, and let the landowner know of the person's name and vehicle description.

Landowners often worry about personal injury to visitors, and if you offer to write up a notice which states that you take all the risk, your chance of gaining access may increase. Lawsuits frighten everyone, and it will help if you take the burden off the property owner.

If you are able to have a conversation with a landowner, it will help to reassure them that you are aware of the important items. Explain that you will not drive or walk through unharvested fields; you will not shoot near livestock or dwellings; you abide by all game laws; you do not damage fences; you are aware of the property boundaries; you do not bring alcohol along and do not litter the land with trash. Last, it will help if you tell the landowner that you will watch for others who may stray onto the property.

After you have received permission, ask the landowner if they would mind giving written consent for your protection. Be sure to contact them again if you wish to continue hunting there in a future season.

Many hunters frown upon others who lease land for the right to hunt. Unfortunately, however, it has occurred all over the country, and in some states it has nearly reached the epidemic state. You either lease land or don't hunt private farms.

A few years ago, I joined in with four others on a hunting lease. I did not particularly favor leasing land, nor do I now. I would much rather hunt without paying, but land in that area was slowly being leased. It appeared certain that an area we had all hunted for several years, with permission, would soon follow. We assumed it was a matter of leasing the property or losing it forever.

Both pros and cons exist regarding leasing land. Naturally, the good includes the opportunity to scout and hunt the area without being interfered with by others. Sometimes this will increase the opportunity for success considerably. It also gives you the opportunity to wait for a trophy buck, or to do what it takes in the area to establish trophies, without other hunters interfering. The right nutritional foods can sometimes be planted to help antler growth, and to keep the deer in the area.

No doubt, a lot of trophy bucks are taken on private land where a minimum amount of hunting pressure exists. Minimal hunting pressure also allows your hunting skills to have a greater bearing upon your success rate, rather than merely hoping someone else pushes deer to you.

The cost of leasing ground may help you decide quickly whether you should participate. In many areas this has ranged from 25 cents to several dollars per acre. And sometimes, regardless of the cost, the idea of having to pay bothers us the most.

Some have monopolized hunting areas simply because of wealth. They offer big money to several landowners in a given area, and wind up with more than they, their friends and relatives can hunt in a lifetime.

I don't believe any *right* or *wrong* exists when it comes to leasing ground. Nowadays, you may have to do it to hunt in some areas. Still, I hope some parcels of private land will remain open to those seeking permission, simply because it will help our future generations.

Some post their land, "Hunting by permission only." Although this appears to spell good news for the hunter who reads it, no guarantee exists. Many times the landowner prefers to screen hunters first, and rightfully so.

Wildlife resources on public lands provide many economic benefits to this country. According to the U.S. Department of the Interior, hunters spend more than 5 million days, and $145 million in economic benefits on public lands. The Bureau of Land Management (BLM) manages habitat covering nearly

Public areas may be crowded early, but offer excellent potential late in the season.

one third of a billion acres. This land is home for more than 3,000 species of mammals, birds, reptiles, fish and amphibians.

Wildlife biologists use the term *carrying capacity* when determining how many animals a given area can support. Several factors, such as cover, food and water play roles in deciding this. If the proper habitat in an area increases, so might the carrying capacity.

With a little imagination, one also could use the term *carrying capacity* when determining the number of deer hunters a particular area can hold. In many special hunt areas, game and fish departments regulate both hunter numbers and bag limits. In the case of some public lands, however, any number of hunters can participate. This often leads to interference and an overcrowded woods, which has caused many to lease land or seek permission from a landowner for hunting privileges.

For some reason, though, something about a **No Trespassing** sign grabs our attention. I guess the desire to venture where we have not yet been can bring out the Daniel Boone in all of us.

CHAPTER 2

HUNTING THE FOOD SOURCES

A good insight of the whitetail's food preference in your area, and when they prefer certain foods, can play a major role in your success. The whitetail bucks, like the does and yearlings, may visit a particular food source regularly during portions of the archery and gun seasons. If the hunter is aware of the preferred foods, they can utilize them at chosen times.

I do not hunt food sources consistently. Other hunting techniques are much more reliable when several foods are available to the whitetail, which is the case in many farmland areas. But I do concentrate on which foods the whitetail prefers any time during the season, and then apply them to obvious hunting methods. These may include hunting rub lines, scrapes or simply waiting in ambush along a well-used trail.

There are times, though, that I do rely solely on food sources to hunt bucks. These instances generally occur during the mid-winter period or archery and muzzleloading seasons. There is normally an abundance of food during the early archery

archery or firearm season in most states. However, your chances of success when hunting the food sources depend not only on the availability of food, but also the amount of hunting pressure and number of bucks in a given area.

The whitetail prefers those foods that offer nutritional supplements of protein and carbohydrates.

Deer eat a wide variety of green plants, leaves and twigs, when available. In tough winters a high browse line may be noticeable, and the hard winters can kill the weakest because of food availability. Many northern hunters capitalize when heavy snow forces the deer to move at any hour of the day to locate food. They may not be hunting a food source, but they will see more deer simply because of increased deer movement.

The whitetail prefers several foods, but they tend to choose those that offer the nutritional supplements. When foods that offer the necessary protein or carbohydrates are not available, they turn to less nutritional foods.

Fall and winter foods are most critical because they affect body condition and winter survival. Unlike the agricultural fields that many hunters believe the most important, buds, twigs and leaves of shrubs and trees are essential. If the hunter can learn about those in the area they hunt, they will increase their chances of spotting bucks.

In 1970-71, the Pennsylvania Game Commission in cooperation with the Pennsylvania State University Wildlife Research Unit, used stomach content analysis techniques to determine seasonal uses of foods by whitetails in seven regions.

Plants, or parts thereof, identified in the stomach content samples were placed under *Woody Plants* or *Non-Woody Plants*. The final analysis found that deer had ate 57 different woody plants and 41 various non-woody plants.

According to an article published by Pennsylvania Game News, authored by Stephen A. Liscinsky, Charles T. Cushwa, Michael J. Puglisi and Michael A. Ondik, the use of leaves from woody plants revealed red maple, cherry, blueberry, grape and oak were the most prevalent in summer, while hemlock, laurel and pine were more prevalent in the winter.

Apples and acorns were important fruits. The analysis demonstrated the use of apples were high, as were acorns. Other

A Pennsylvania study showed that a deer will utilize many foods.

fruits, such as cherry, blueberry, grape and blackberry were present, too.

Non-woody plants ranged from common crops like alfalfa, corn, oats, clover, wheat and soybeans, to lesser common foods such as strawberry, cantaloupe, dandelion, pokeweed and goldenrod.

According to the survey, seasonal differences in foods were found to be greater than regional differences. About 60 percent of the yearly diet consisted of woody plants. The importance of woody stems, leaves and fruit changed with both seasons and regions. Leaves were a more important year-round food, with evergreen utilization increasing when deciduous leaves were less available.

The analysis indicated that deer choose from what is available. The summary concluded that deer utilize many foods, but their choices are governed by the succulence and palatability of whatever is available at a given time.

With this in mind, any hunter can realize the potential of hunting food sources at particular times of the year. One example could be noted from a farmer and biologist in Iowa. To most hunters, corn is corn. We know deer like to eat the golden kernels, and there are hunting opportunities when corn is available. However, a wildlife biologist with the Iowa DNR recently examined a cornfield of a different genetic strain. They call it *high lysine* corn, and the deer apparently prefer it to other corn. Evidence showed the deer had mutilated several areas of the field to get to the high lysine corn. The Iowa DNR often plants the corn in areas that may attract the deer away from other farmer's crop fields. Thus far, no studies have been conducted to see why the high lysine corn is favored above others.

I hunt various agricultural foods, but do so only when they are hot. One example is corn. A harvested cornfield normally attracts deer on a regular basis 10 to 15 days after the harvest. Of course, this varies according to the availability of other foods and whether or not the field is plowed for the following season. After the active period, I go back to other hunting techniques. But if the corn is harvested during or near the rut, the bucks will be there, either to feed or look for estrous does.

Soybeans do not interest me after the hunting season begins. Seldom are the beans green and offering a tasty handout to the whitetails. But I do watch the soybeans during August when they attract deer regularly. Even though the hunting has not yet begun, the soybeans tell me what bucks are in the area, and enable me to locate nearby rub lines after the season begins.

This mid-winter buck is preparing to dine on lush winter wheat, a favored late season food source.

Clover and alfalfa are excellent food sources during the fall and winter months. And if these areas do not receive a great deal of hunting pressure, you don't have to worry that every buck in the area could be totally nocturnal.

Winter wheat does little for me in the Midwest until December, though several states consider it a favored whitetail food source. In the preceding months other foods tend to overrule the wheat. But after Jack Frost visits the area several times, the wheat becomes a common food source. When snow accumulates a few inches, but not enough to cover a rich wheat field, the deer become even more regular.

To hunt bucks successfully near agricultural fields requires an understanding of their habits in a particular area. If they receive a lot of hunting pressure, you probably will need to hunt closer to the bedding areas. Other factors, such as wind direction and distance between the bedding areas and food sources, will affect your buck hunting. If you fail to recognize the wind direction, there is little chance in succeeding. The key is to have several locations and hunt only those that keep your scent blowing away from the bedding areas. If there is a considerable amount of distance between the bedding and feeding areas, perhaps a 1/4 mile or more, it also will affect your chances of success. The buck can travel several trails to reach the food sources, and there is little chance you will be along the right trail.

If you do not hunt a pressured area, you can concentrate your efforts closer to the agricultural fields. The bucks are more likely to reach them before dark, and may provide a shooting opportunity. However, determining exactly where a buck will enter a field is not easily accomplished. For the gun hunter, it may or may not matter, but for the bowhunter it is vitally important.

I have hunted on the edges of crop fields on many occasions, and have not come up with a sure-fire method for determining where a certain buck will enter. This holds true on the same bucks that I have seen enter a field on numerous occasions. I sincerely believe the best chance, though, is to pick one ambush location and stick with it when the wind is favorable. Eventually, the buck may pass by you at close yardage. And if a buck begins to enter a field from the same general location, I will waste no time in moving a stand to that area.

When hunting an agricultural food source, I do not prefer to place a stand on the edge. When the light of day subsides, you become a silhouette against the skyline. An

The red and white oaks can be distinguished by the pointed or rounded lobes of the leaves. Illus. by Larry Smail.

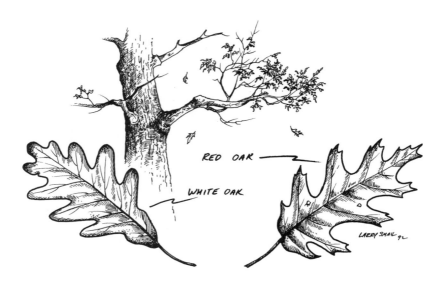

approaching buck is sure to spot your movement, and spoil a perfect opportunity. Moving into the timber, at least 20 to 40 yards, will help providing you can utilize a background. Whether it is leaves, trees or limbs, the natural surroundings will help you stay hidden.

Of the deciduous oaks, two groups are widely distributed in North America. Both the red oak and white oak family provide staple foods for the whitetail. Acorns are probably the number one food source in most states, and will help with antler growth.

The eastern half of the country is blessed with both groups, although the red oak family may extend further westward than the white oaks. A close observation of the leaves will allow you to separate them easily. The leaves of oaks in the white oak family have rounded lobes, while the red oak leaves are pointed.

White oaks are more popular with whitetails in the earlier fall months because they ripen sooner than the red oaks,

The sweet taste of white oak acorns often attracts deer early in the season. However, the location of the oak may affect the time of visitation.

and offer a sweeter taste. I do not hunt white oaks regularly, but they can provide the hunter with action when only a few of the trees produce a large nut mast. When there are several white oaks in a given area, and all produce a bumper-crop of acorns, the hunter will not usually do as well. The over-abundance of food makes it difficult to determine which tree will offer the best hunting opportunities. However, the bucks will benefit tremendously, and so will your hunting area.

I often hunt black or pin oaks during the winter months. The bitter acorns do not attract deer frequently like the white oak acorns, but they will visit the trees consistently when other food sources are not available.

In areas where logging has occurred, the hunter can look for smaller white and red oaks that have not been removed. These trees were left behind because of little value, but will often produce enough acorns to keep deer coming in regularly. In the remaining chapters I will discuss several methods for hunting oaks in both the early and late seasons.

Newly logged areas should always be considered, particularly one year following the timber cutting. I am not overly-fond of tree cutting in areas where it has not been regulated, but the new growth offers excellent foods for deer.

Perhaps the most undesirable factor of hunting cut-over areas are their appearance. They leave much to be desired when it comes to looks. And if you are looking for a tree to hang your stand, you may become even more frustrated. But their thick vegetation also offers excellent bedding areas, thus providing sufficient habitat.

I really enjoy hunting bucks in the hidden food sources. They really aren't hidden, but few hunters look at these foods as a hunting possibility.

The falling pods of the honeylocust has provided me with several hunting opportunities. These trees are common from the eastern side of the Dakotas to the Appalachian Mountains in the east, and from the Canadian border to the southern tip of the gulf states. The trees reach heights of 75 feet or more, and tend to grow in moist, fertile soils. Their pods are dark,

Woody Williams took this respectable Indiana buck while hunting in a cut-over area.

reddish brown, about 8 to 12 inches long, 1 inch wide, and begin falling in the fall months. Although the pod contains seeds, I am unsure if the deer feed on them for this reason, or for the succulent pods.

The most difficult part of hunting hidden food sources is locating them. You have to know what types of food sources are available in your area, and how to recognize them. Several fine books are now available that offer descriptive definitions and excellent illustrations of the plants and trees which provide food during the fall months. Many of these publications can be found at your local library.

All deer hunters have probably heard or witnessed deer eating apples. Only a few hunters are fortunate to have these delicious fruits growing near home, but many do have sour crab apples nearby. When domestic apples can't be found, crab apple trees provide a favored food source.

Crab apple trees usually grow around mature fields, thickets, old roadbeds and near the edges of tall timber. Their thorn-like twigs make them easy to spot, as does the small yellow-green fruit they bear. Depending on when the first frost occurs, fruits usually begin dropping to the ground sometime in September or October. Deer usually find them quickly. On occasion I have seen them stand on their hind legs to eat apples before they have begun falling.

Four years ago I hunted a secluded stand of crab apple trees during the early portion of the archery season. Only two of the six or seven trees were bearing fruit, but it was enough to attract a wide eight-pointer. The rut was still several weeks away, and had it not been for the hidden crabs, I seriously doubt I would have known he existed. He reached me just before dark and came for the sole reason of feeding on any available apples.

Most berries, whether they are the bramble types such as blackberries, or the delicious blueberry and cranberry kinds, provide food for the whitetail only in the summer months. The dogwood, however, produces its red berry fruit in the fall and winter, which can quickly become a hidden food source for many species of wildlife, including deer.

The easiest way to locate dogwoods is to see them in the spring when their flowering ritual is peaking. In the fall and winter you must look for them in well-drained areas, paying close attention to trees that are short and full. Though the leaves may have fallen, the trees are somewhat thick because of the large quantity of limbs they produce. More than 15 species of dogwoods exist across the country.

Of all the hidden foods, honeysuckle may be overlooked more than other types. I assume because of its availability, it is

This button buck may feed on the honeylocust pods daily until the supply is exhausted.

35

often taken for granted. In my earlier hunting experiences, I never considered it a huntable food origin because of its over-abundance in nearly every area I hunted. I simply passed by, thinking of the thick vines only as a good location for deer to bed. Not until I witnessed it did I believe that the deer relied on the lush green foliage for winter food.

Unlike other plants and trees, the honeysuckle holds its leaves in the winter months. The plant will darken, becoming pale and dull in appearance, but its green leaves offer both taste and nutrition for the whitetail. Because of this, I prefer to hunt near honeysuckle thickets late in the season. It is generally prime in most areas during early December or later. After several nights of freezing temperatures, other food sources begin to dwindle. Acorns are not nearly as plentiful, and the green foliage of other plants have vanished for another year.

I spend time chasing cottontails in January. When snow is on the ground I concentrate on the areas offering cover, such as honeysuckle. However, after seeing so much deer sign, I am convinced they favor the thick vegetation as much as the rabbits.

Mushrooms are an important part of the deer's diet in certain parts of the country. They grow in dark, moist areas where other plants requiring light cannot grow. If deer are passing through the area regularly, you can bet they will feed on the mushrooms.

A few years ago my son, John, located an area in the middle of a thicket that was overrun with deer sign. He had no explanation why the deer were concentrated in the small area, but it seemed worthwhile to find a reason.

A short time later we walked into the area. At first I saw no logical food offering that would attract the deer, but the reason soon became obvious. I looked up to investigate the skinny, tall trees surrounding us and my heart skipped a couple of beats. Each tree was covered in golfball-size persimmons.

Although there were hundreds of the hanging fruits above us, the deer had kept the ground cleaned up. The persimmon thicket had become a daily stopover and a prime food source.

We moved the tree stand into the persimmon trees, and the following morning a small buck entered the thicket. After a few minutes of browsing, the buck turned, offering the shot all bowhunters wait for. Five deer were taken from the persimmon thicket in two years, including a respectable 8-pointer.

Although this incident occurred several years ago, it marked the start of my search for hidden food sources. I say *hidden* because these types of food offerings are always found away from the usual fields that surround our hunting areas. Many of us feel gifted we can hunt near harvested corn, soybeans, clover, barley and other prime food origins, but these potential hot spots seldom last. They may pay off early in the season, during a peak period, but most always subside quickly.

The biggest advantage of hunting hidden food sources is the time of day deer visit them. As a rule, these places are found in the thickest cover close to bedding areas, thus making it more likely for them to arrive later in the morning and earlier in the evening.

These secluded food plots also can pay off during the rut. Bucks, as I have discovered, will make consistent visits if the does and fawns remain regular. Both rubs and scrapes begin showing up as the rut intensifies, as do the number of bucks passing through.

After my son took the buck from the persimmon thicket, I made it a point to locate another. Shortly before the rut I discovered such a place a half-mile from where he had hunted. There were four of the trees in a 40 yard circle and all contained persimmons.

After putting up the blind and seeing no buck sign, I assumed my chances of scoring were slim. However, one week later a new scrape and several rubs appeared under the persimmon trees. In the days that followed I spotted six different bucks that had come into the food source hoping to find a cooperative doe. The best was an 8-pointer that sported a 15-inch spread. Although I never managed to get a clean shot, it was enjoyable to see how he and the other bucks responded to the area. Seldom would they feed on the available persimmons. The does and fawns did each day as they passed through, but the bucks came in only to use their nose.

Your area will no doubt have hidden food sources, providing you can locate them. Several more that can provide hunting opportunities are as follows: beechnuts, teaberry, snowberry, white pine, yellow birch, sumac, sassafras, elderberry, black cherry, poplar and willow.

Surprisingly, maples provide a great deal of nutrition for the whitetail. Both the leaves and buds provide the necessary proteins when available.

When the whitetail faces starvation, it will turn to spruce, balsam fir, red pine and Jack pine.

A great deal of emphasis has been placed on hunting bucks over scrapes, but I believe food sources offer as much or more chance for success. In early fall, bucks feed routinely like does. They may not be as frequent, but they still feed at various times in daylight hours. When the rut is in full swing, bucks widen their travel routes in search of does. When the rut begins to subside, bucks again become more routine; their normal pattern returns to some extent. This continues bringing them to the food source, offering an opportunity for the late season hunter. Winter days become shorter and food availability decreases, which often narrows the buck's range.

Because factors can change quickly, the best method to locating food sources is persistent scouting. All food sources are generally hot at the beginning, but cool off as time passes. You

Hidden food sources, such as honeysuckle and persimmons may appear desirable to a buck. They often offer seclusion, which can bring a buck into the area during the daylight hours.

also should check with your local game and fish departments to get the inside information on favored foods. There is a good possibility they have performed studies regarding this in your area.

Through studies we know a whitetail requires at least 15 percent protein in its daily diet. Many wild foods do not supply the necessary protein and nutrition needed, but this does not mean the whitetail won't feed on a particular source. Specific foods attract deer at certain times of the year, and you can bet the same food will attract deer the following year if it is available.

CHAPTER 3

FUNNELS AND SMALL WOODLOTS

I seldom get enthusiastic about hunting a small woodlot surrounded on all sides by agricultural fields. Nor do I get fired up when I locate a narrow funnel that has sunlit openings on two sides. But I do know that many of these areas have potential if the hunter can push themselves into spending time there.

Trophy deer come out of these small areas every season, as do several 1 1/2-year-old bucks. All deer are attracted to them for various reasons. Some, however, do rate better than others, and locating these hotspots will make any hunter want to look for another.

I know of one funnel that has produced several bucks in the last 10 years. It has been a favorite hunting location for myself and several hunting companions. Although none of the bucks harvested in the area have made the record book, a few have been very respectable. Even more impressive is the number of bucks seen that were not taken. And had the area not

41

A topographic or aerial map will help you locate productive funnels and woodlots.

been stripped of its timber a few months prior to writing this book, I would be looking forward to hunting there again.

This funnel was a connecting link between a bedding area and food source. It was the only cover available that would allow the deer to move back and forth without exposing them. If they chose to travel either side of the funnel, they would be forced to walk the open fields.

Funnels also provide escape routes, and I would assume a buck does not have a fear of bedding close to the funnel. They know the funnel will provide them with a hidden travel route. Those who like to drive deer can utilize a funnel to their advantage, too.

Oaks, or any other food source may attract deer to a funnel. But this is not what makes a particular area better than another year after year.

Funnels are attractive to bucks during the rut because they offer them a hidden line of travel. Their home range expands considerably, and they will use any bottleneck to their advantage, simply because it links them with another area in a comfortable manner.

The author ambushed this small buck during the black powder season as the deer traveled a funnel to reach his bedding area.

Small woodlots are similar to funnels, except they do not connect to other enticing areas where the deer may want to feed and bed. A small woodlot is productive when there is little or no deer/human interference, and a bedding area is offered where food is nearby.

Most hunters do not pay attention to small woodlots. I assume this is human nature. We all like hunting bigger pockets of timber, and feel more confident that something will walk by. When we enter a woodlot and see daylight surrounding each side, we naturally become discouraged.

I have hunted in the farmlands of Alberta, Canada where many woodlots varied from 3 or 4 acres to several times that amount. I quickly learned, though, that any woodlot offered excellent potential when the right conditions existed. It seemed

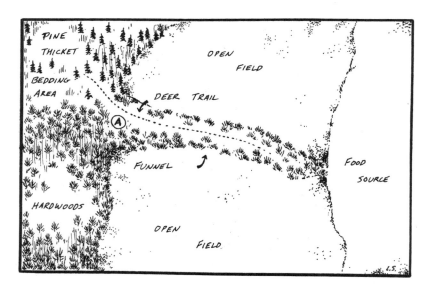

In this case it would be better to place the stand at Point A. This would allow the deer to reach you earlier in the evenings and later in the mornings. Illus. by Larry Smail.

This funnel may offer potential at Point A and Point B. Bucks will travel the funnel during the rut while expanding their range. Illus. by Larry Smail.

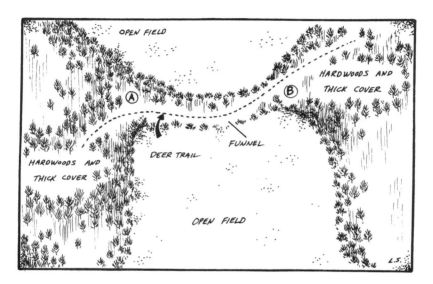

that any of the small woodlots held a few deer (including a buck) if a food source was nearby. The deer may have entered the food source from different locations each evening when they left the woodlot, but they would usually return to the same woodlot each day to bed.

Locating a productive funnel or woodlot can be a difficult task. Leg work is essential, along with driving roads whenever available. However, maps offer the quickest and easiest method.

Both topographic and aerial photo maps will provide you with the best look at a given area. I prefer the aerial maps, but they are not as easy to obtain. Topos are much easier to come by, but they are often outdated and may not give a true layout of the territory.

Funnels often run along fence lines or ditches. They are any grown-up area that connects on one, or both ends to a larger stand of timber or cover. They can be several hundred yards wide, or extremely narrow, but either can produce results when the proper conditions exist.

The productive funnel mentioned earlier in this chapter was no more than 75 yards wide. The narrower bottlenecks are excellent choices, simply because you can cover them better. That is what makes one funnel more exceptional than another. However, it does not mean that any funnel will draw bucks.

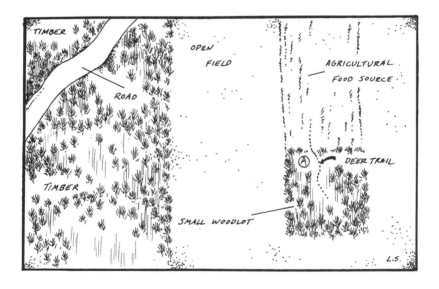

The small woodlot on the right could provide an opportunity. This may serve as a buck's hideout away from the hunting pressure. Point A would make a good ambush location.

Anytime during the hunting season offers an excellent opportunity to hunt a funnel. If there is a food source that the bucks may be coming to, then the funnel probably will be a natural area for them to pass through regularly. If there is nothing to attract the bucks, the funnel may be dead until the rut is in full swing. Bucks will use it then because it is handy and provides protection for them to travel from one area to another.

You also should keep in mind that all deer like to travel the easiest routes. Many times a bottleneck will provide them with this convenience.

I know of one area that was grown-up in tall timber throughout the funnel. Although it was somewhat open with very little cover, the deer used it regularly because both sides of the funnel were overgrown with blackberry and other bramble bushes. The deer would often browse in and out of the thorny areas, or use it for bedding, but they used the bottleneck between them to travel from one end to the other. They would have been hidden much better in the large sections of thickets, but instead they traveled the easy route.

Of the smaller woodlots, I prefer those located away from the roads. I have spent many hours in the vehicle watching a small woods from several hundred yards away just to see what might come out of it to feed in the evenings. And if the woods is hidden from the road, I walk as close as necessary, making it a point to go unnoticed.

Many small woodlots become escapes for bucks when the hunting pressure increases. This is because few hunters venture into them, before and during the season. I like hunting there anytime during the season, though, simply because I usually have them to myself.

The most difficult part of hunting small woodlots is getting in and out without creating a disturbance. I always plan my approach and departure accordingly to keep from being spotted or scented. If a buck is leaving the woodlot on the east side in the afternoons, for example, I come in from the east and leave on the west. I always make it a point to avoid walking through the small woods. Ordinarily I will circle the woods when I need to leave on the opposite side.

When setting up a stand on a small woodlot, I always keep it near the edge. I don't believe it is worth taking a risk.

I recall one small woods where I placed my stand about ten yards inside the edge. After a two hour wait, I spotted movement about 70 yards into the woods. Instantly I saw antlers and I knew the buck was coming. I remember how amazed I was that the buck seemed to appear out of nowhere. Unfortunately, the 2-year-old buck passed by me just out of bow range when he entered a section of honeysuckle that butted against the small woods.

Whenever I hunt a funnel, I place my stand wherever it appears it will do the most good. If I am bowhunting and the bottleneck is narrow, I may set up in the middle if I can shoot to the nearby edge on each side. Ordinarily, one excellent trail will be visible. I seldom set up my stand right beside the trail, though, unless the funnel is extremely wide.

Since most funnels tend to be wider on the ends, I concentrate on the center. There is less chance that a buck can get by, and again more possibility of getting a shot. However, the total length of the bottleneck also should be taken into consideration. If it is several hundred yards long, with a food source at one end and a bedding area located near the other, I place my stand accordingly. Normally I prefer to hunt closer to the bedding area in both the morning and evening. A deer can spend a long time traveling a short distance, and I prefer not to have to wait any longer than necessary.

Funnels and small woodlots should not be considered the only way to hunt. But they can become the key to locating bucks that you never knew existed.

CHAPTER 4

THE EARLY ARCHERY SEASON

Many states open their archery season before the summer has ended, or so it seems. Most think of it as Indian summer, and it brings warm days, numerous bugs, and not as cool of nights as we would prefer.

From the non-hunters point of view, it can mean the chance at one last weekend picnic before the cold days start rolling in. However, the deer hunter looks at it much differently. He or she knows it will affect deer movement, and cause a great inconvenience when and if a deer is taken. During the first few days of the season, though, it does not mean that bucks are not vulnerable. As a matter of fact, I believe the first week of the archery season is often the best.

I have always been a record keeper. For as many years as I have hunted whitetails, I have kept statistics that showed how many deer, what kind of deer, and when the deer were seen.

Surprisingly, records from the first week boasted the highest number of sightings. The totals even showed that bucks moved freely early in the season, and in some cases these figures were as high as the same number of days during the peak of the rut. I really don't need the records to tell me this, however.

My past experiences have relayed this message on numerous occasions. One of my best, along with several other smaller bucks, were taken during early October only a few days into the season.

My experiences have also indicated that the buck movement goes downhill rapidly after the first week of hunting. The second and third weeks never compared to the first, even though the temperatures were usually considerably cooler and more suitable to the bow hunter. In the later weeks, though, buck movement increased as the rut progressed.

The lack of hunting pressure is one reason a buck is not so nocturnal early in the season. They are not used to frequent confrontations with man, nor has our scent been spread along every trail. This occurs after we have begun hunting, and continues until the hunting pressure subsides.

Bucks in farming areas are gifted to have the availability of so many food sources. The fields generally begin drawing deer long before the season opens. The bucks, like the does and fawns, have become programed to feed before dark because of the long summer days. Although the actual feeding times can vary depending on the area and amount of disturbance, most bucks will still feed during the daylight hours in the months of July, August and September.

In one area of Indiana where I spend several days hunting each year, control permits allow landowners to kill a designated number of deer. This begins in late July and continues through part of August. It is not surprising for me to watch the same fields in late August and early September, and see bucks come out before dark. Somehow the bucks don't seem to place the depredation period as the hunting period. Perhaps

The author's father locates an early season buck rub.

that is because most of the depredation takes place in the fields. We are not bumping into them like we do during the season, and our scent is not left on a regular basis. Of course, whenever several bucks are taken in one particular area by someone using problem deer control permits, there is going to be a difference in the number of bucks that come to the field. I am just trying to get the point across that farmland bucks in many areas still practice late summer habits close to the time the bowhunting begins.

I am not one to scout during every month of the year. I do spend several days of every month in the outdoors, but my purpose is not always to prepare for the next deer season. In the winter months I am trying to call in coyotes and foxes. As spring approaches I begin turkey scouting and hunting. Even during the hot days of summer, I spend time pursuing woodchucks or photographing wildlife. However, deer are always on my mind and I pay close attention to whatever sign is there.

Some hunters claim that winter scouting, just after the deer hunting ends, provides an excellent opportunity to locate bucks for the next season. Perhaps the area plays a role in the effectiveness of post-season scouting, but I have not found it is that helpful. I always have this inner-feeling that the rub or scrape was made by a buck that has already entered the *land of no return*. After all, if the sign was not fresh, who can say if the buck is still around.

I prefer to start scouting seriously in the late summer. One helpful tactic is to see what is there. Spotlighting is legal in Indiana as long as you don't bring along a weapon. Many states, however, have prohibited the use of a spotlight, and I would recommend you first check the regulations where you live. But if it is legal, the deer hunter can locate bucks by driving roads, concentrating on soybean fields, alfalfa, harvested corn or any other agricultural food source.

At this time of year a buck moves very little. You can bet that a buck you see one hour after dark did not come from far away. The overall distance between the food source and their bedding area is sure to be very little.

Although I locate several bucks every year using the spotlighting technique, my favorite method is to arrive on a selected field a couple of hours before dark. In cases where a field is accessible by road, I park the vehicle and wait. My preference, though, is to walk along the field's edge until I have located a point where the visibility is good. I want to see as much in one evening as possible so that too much time isn't wasted at a particular location.

A good pair of binoculars is essential, particularly if you watch a big field. This enables you to see antlers when and if deer enter the field from several hundred yards away. Bucks are

The author scouts in the early season by watching fields. The bucks often visit them in the evening before dusk.

often traveling together in the late summer, and it is not uncommon to see several in one bunch if you position yourself on the right field.

Depending on the number of deer I see from a selected field, I try not to spend too much time in one place. If I sit on a field until dark, and the weather is ideal for deer movement, I limit myself to two or three visitations. If I have not spotted bucks during that time, I move on to another area. And if I do see bucks, I make notes of how many, where they entered the field, and estimate their scoring potential. When I feel I have gained this valuable information, I move on to another field. By starting early, I have plenty of room for error. It is always my hope to locate three or four promising areas before opening day arrives.

I consider a soybean field the best candidate for bringing bucks in during July and August. However, since they usually turn brown from the summer's heat in late August, I watch them only to see what bucks are in the area. By the time September rolls around the bucks are not likely to be feeding there, unless nothing else is available.

When I select a field, I do an evaluation to see where I should sit. This is done early in the afternoon before the deer

Any pre-season scouter would appreciate locating these bucks.

move. The last thing I want is to let the deer know I am there, which could cause a major change in habits.

If the field is flat, I can be comfortable sitting about anywhere. If the area is hilly, I prefer to pick a high point to allow the best visibility.

When walking the edge of the field, I locate the most promising trails. Deer are creatures of habit in the late summer, and you can count on them to consistently use the same trails to enter a field. On many fields I come to know some deer quite well. There are regulars that tend to come out about the same time and location every afternoon.

After locating the well-used trails, I position myself far away to keep from being scented or seen. I carry along a fold-up stool and simply move into the brush a few feet from the field's edge. The vegetation is still green and thick, and seldom do I need any other camouflage to conceal me.

When I arrive at a field, I park my vehicle where it will not create a disturbance when I leave. This can often mean walking a little farther, but it is well worth the exercise.

I also think about my departure whenever I set up. I prefer to stay close to the vehicle so there is less field to walk, and less chance of running off deer along the way. On some occasions I have had to postpone leaving until long after dark, just to keep from spooking bucks.

A few years ago I had watched a 10-pointer on three different evenings. The Pope & Young candidate was consistent when entering the soybean field. He always came in to the field about 150 yards north of where I sat, and always left the field just before dark. I could leave by walking the edge back to the south, and never had to worry about alarming him. However, I returned just to see him one more time. The big buck came out just before dark within 100 yards of my position, and spent what daylight was left browsing closer. It was 30 minutes after dark when I finally left, assuming the deer had moved on. But the instant I began walking I heard a deer run into the nearby cover. I never saw the buck again.

I don't believe you can get by with making mistakes when it comes to hunting trophy bucks. They have a tendency to wise up quickly, particularly when the rut is not affecting their movements.

When the archery season is about to begin, I concentrate on using two techniques for hunting bucks. One very good method is hunting rubs, or rub lines. The following chapter will discuss how to locate effective rub lines before and after the rut begins.

Southern Indiana bowhunter Mark Williams uses a topographic map to locate bedding areas and food sources. Topos may save unnecessary leg work.

The other method is to hunt the food sources, and there are two times of the year to do it; early in the archery season, and during the winter just before the season closes.

I have already covered food sources from different regions, and you probably already know the popular early season foods in your area from personal experience. The food source is important to bucks at this time of year because they are storing fat for the rut period. This will provide them with needed energy, and allow them to spend their time chasing after does.

As mentioned earlier in this chapter, soybeans seldom become a reliable food source in the early fall. Once harvested, though, it can become a regular offering when nothing else is available. Late in the season this can change. As other food sources dry up, the stubbles left in the soybean field again become a favorite.

If you locate a newly harvested cornfield just prior to the season's opener, you have probably found a gold mine. In my opinion, nothing attracts all deer any better than a field full of yellow pebbles. Many harvests do vary, though, and scouting is necessary to find out how effective the field is. Some farmers plow their fields after harvesting. These fields will not attract as many deer, simply because the food is not as plentiful. Other fields may be full of corn and attract the same deer, including the bucks, every day until the food source dwindles.

Most harvested cornfields will attract deer for long periods of time, but the first few days provide the best hunting opportunity. After a week or so, the deer do not visit the area as frequently, nor do they arrive as promptly.

One example of this occurred during the deer season just prior to the writing of this book. My son hunted a newly placed stand about 40 yards from the edge of a cornfield that the farmer picked the previous day. On the first evening he spotted three different bucks, and numerous does and fawns. The following

HUNTING FARMLAND BUCKS

By hunting close to a buck's bedding area, you will be more likely to intercept them during daylight hours.

afternoon he again saw three bucks, and several other deer. The next day he saw two bucks, and missed one within bow range. The stand did not get hunted again until I visited it a few days later. I saw only a doe and fawn, and neither of us managed to cash in on the opportunity.

A lot should be taken into consideration when setting up a stand along a harvested cornfield, or any other agricultural food source. Most often I do not like to place the stand along the field's edge, simply because I don't want to rely on a buck being out in the open before dark. I prefer to be located somewhere inside the brush, but just how far depends on hunting pressure, the nocturnal habits of the bucks, and the location of the bedding area.

In Alberta, well-known whitetail hunter and guide, Jim Hole, rarely hunts anywhere except the edge of a field. The area is a bow-zone only, and little pressure exists. Although the big boys are practically nocturnal, they will, and often do enter the alfalfa fields just before dark. Hole prefers not to set up inside the brush and timber to avoid spooking the bucks. Many of the woodlots are small and the bucks often bed close to the fields. His techniques have worked very well. He has taken several trophies, and so have his clients.

In many areas this method doesn't work. If a hunter would spend every evening sitting on the edge of a field, he or she would be lucky to see a big buck during the entire season, simply because they avoid the open.

I have hunted close to the edge, though, and have managed to see bucks on a regular basis, even though they practice the nocturnal habits. A buck feels somewhat safer anytime it is in cover. He may work slowly to a field, and spend the last 30 minutes of daylight browsing just off the edge waiting for darkness to arrive.

The main factor that determines how early a buck arrives at the food source depends on the bedding area. If your area contains a great deal of dense vegetation, and only a small food source, it is possible the bucks will be bedded a considerable distance away. On the other hand, if there are several open areas, regardless of whether or not they are food sources, the bucks bedding area becomes more limited. He is forced to bed closer simply because there is less to choose from.

The best way to locate a buck's bedding area is to run him out of it. Unfortunately this technique may push him out of the area entirely, forcing him to find a more suitable area that has fewer interruptions. No doubt, there is a great deal of truth in this when it comes to big bucks. I have jumped small bucks and had them return the very next day. Some may have come back

59

Can you see this buck? It is not uncommon for a buck to head for thick cover when the hunting begins.

on the same day, but I was not there to witness the event.

Topographic maps are excellent tools. They will help you with several techniques, including narrowing down the bedding areas.

Bucks like it thick. No matter what state I have hunted in, the bucks always seek the dense cover. And you can bet, if there is only one small pocket of thick cover in a square mile, a buck will use it to his advantage. These can vary according to the locality and the time of the year.

I have seen thick stands of pines serve the same purpose as a one-acre plot of bramble bush and honeysuckle. In the early archery season these areas can change, however, as leaves begin falling and early morning frosts take their toll on the lower vegetation.

When I have found what I believe is a bedding area, I place my stand close by, staying in the thick cover whenever possible. By being close to the beds, I am able to catch bucks moving earlier in the evenings and later in the mornings. And when a buck is nocturnal, this is vitally important.

Many hunters choose to stay close to acorn pockets, particularly when the oaks have a banner year. I seldom select this method for locating bucks because of either the abundance of acorns, or because of the open woods where many white oaks are found. Oaks do not always have a good year, and droughts or other factors can affect the nut crop. When they are plentiful, they provide an excellent needed food source for all deer, but they don't offer the perfect opportunity to take a buck. When acorns are falling to the ground continuously in the early fall, the deer will find the available food anywhere, or so it seems. They don't become reliable at a particular location, and a hunter can kill several days waiting for something to happen.

I often do hunt an isolated acorn pocket, particularly when other food sources can't be found. If there is only one producing white oak in a given area, it will surely be visited regularly if no other agricultural foods are nearby.

These hotspots are often difficult to locate. Although the acorns on the ground offer a clue, droppings will let you know beyond a doubt that the oak is special.

Buck rubs can be found close to the oak whenever a buck or two visits regularly. If they make it a constant stopover, you can bet they will leave their mark close to this food supply, often rubbing the same trees again and again.

Unfortunately, a rare acorn pocket doesn't last long. Any number of deer can clean up the acorns as quickly as they fall when there is not an over-abundance. How long the feeding binge will last depends on the number of acorns, and how soon they begin dropping.

The hunter should be sure the deer still come in regularly before placing their stand. On one occasion I found an outstanding oak only one week prior to the season opener. Droppings surrounded the tree, and at least a dozen buck rubs were plainly visible from the oak. I saw numerous acorns on the ground, and it appeared the supply would never run out. I returned three days before opening weekend and hung my stand within a few yards of the big oak. I considered it to be a cinch when I arrived the first morning, but I climbed down three hours later without seeing a deer.

Your success during the early season depends a lot on what you will put into it. I know of some bowhunters who refuse to hunt early because of the heat, and the fact the rut may be several weeks away. But in my opinion the early season is hard to beat. The bucks have not yet been programed for the hunting season, and the wise hunter can easily take advantage of the food sources and bedding areas.

These does led this buck into a stand of oaks.

CHAPTER 5

RUBS AND RUB LINES

I can remember reading a magazine article a few years ago that focused on hunting scrapes and rubs. A strong emphasis was placed on scrapes, and little importance on rubs. The article implied that rubs only tell you where a buck has been, but scrapes tell you where the buck will soon be.

The effectiveness of hunting scrapes and rubs have been argued for many years. I have had success with both. However, when rubs are fresh and demonstrate a pattern, such as a rub line, I feel they offer the hunter much more opportunity. The difficult task is to identify the meaning of the rubs you find, and determine whether or not the buck is nearby.

The meaning of the rub is also a major debate. Some hunters claim they are only a signpost to mark territories. Others say that bucks rub to show dominance, or simply to sharpen and polish their antlers. One deer hunter claimed that rubs are used to guide the buck during the dark hours. We all know that a buck will rub to remove the velvet when the shedding begins, but this normally offers no hunting opportunity, nor does it guarantee the buck will make a return visit.

From research we have learned that rubs usually occur on trees that offer visual recognition, particular scents and those that appear to hold the scent of the deer's glands when it rubs. These various trees are widely distributed. Pines, cedars, maples and poplar remain favorites. And if they are not available in a given area, a buck will turn to others. I have seen pen-raised bucks rub dogwoods when they were the only trees available. Yet in the wild, at least in my neck of the woods, they seldom rub a dogwood tree even though they are plentiful.

Bucks prefer to rub certain trees. Some of their favorites are pine, maple, willow and poplar.

Though researchers are puzzled by the meaning of the scent left on trees, they speculate it is to warn other bucks and to attract does. We have also witnessed does marking a signpost by rubbing their forehead gland. Both does and bucks have been known to lick rubbed trees, indicating another method of providing scent communication.

Ed Rinehart (right) took this buck on the first morning of the fiirearm season. The deer had left his mark on several trees in the area.

Research has also proven that the mature bucks do most of the rubbing early in the fall season. Many bucks, however, do share the same trees, just as they do scrapes. I have also witnessed bucks that scented a previously rubbed tree before they began rubbing.

When a hunter locates a rub on a large tree, they usually believe that a mature buck was responsible. I, too, used to think that only trophy bucks rubbed trees with large diameters. However, while photographing deer in many parks, and spending countless hours watching and studying penned deer, I can throw that philosophy out the door. Research has also shown that small, 1 1/2-year-old bucks do occasionally rub big trees.

I have raised a buck, penned on two acres of natural habitat. The area contains several small, 1 to 3-inch diameter maples and pines. At 1 1/2 years of age, the buck began rubbing the smaller trees in early August. In September, a few weeks after the velvet had been removed, he showed aggression by rubbing several willows around a nearby pond that were four inches or larger. Many of the rubs were quite long. I should add, he carried a 5-inch spike on the right, and a 6-inch antler with a fork on the left side. The 3-pointer, as the rut progressed, even did a minimal amount of rubbing on one of the fence posts that had a diameter of 10 inches.

I do believe, though, that the overall destruction of the tree may represent the size of the buck that visited the area. Long rubs do not necessarily mean a big buck is present, but when you find deeply gouged and fragmented trees it usually indicates that a mature buck is responsible. I have never witnessed a small-antlered buck tearing into a tree the way that many mature bucks have done. But this does not mean that I don't look for large rubs. On the contrary, like most deer hunters, I become excited when I locate large rubs. My vigorous attention often leads to selecting an ambush location nearby.

Rub lines normally begin a few weeks prior to the peak of the rutting season.

To hunt rubs successfully, you must be able to determine whether or not the rubs are consistent. The location of the rubs, as well as their pattern and closeness will make or break your chance of spotting him, or other bucks in the same area that have left their mark.

I never hunt a single, rubbed tree. Many times, if I happen to be perched in a tree stand overlooking a trail, there will be a rub within sight. This is a sign a buck has passed through, but has no bearing on whether or not he will return. However, when rubs create a line, they offer possibilities. I consider a rub line very promising when I can stand near one rub and look to the next. Sometimes I may have to expand my search because of brush and terrain, but there will usually be another connecting rub somewhere close by.

Just how far the line extends, or how far apart each rub is from the next, will vary. I have followed several rub lines that covered several hundred yards, while others could not be followed more than 100 yards. Bedding and feeding areas may affect the distance. Most individual rubs will be spaced no more than 30 to 100 yards apart, but again several conditions will make a difference. However, any rub line is worth hunting, in my opinion. It is a definite sign that a buck has passed through more than once, and a good sign that he will do it again sometime in the future. And as time progresses, there is a good possibility that more rubs will occur along the same line.

Rub lines tend to appear frequently at two times during the year. In the late summer (or early fall in some areas), scattered rubs are often found, but it is rare to locate a rub line during this period. They do not offer much hunting opportunity, even if the archery season begins early. These rubs are due to velvet removing and do not necessarily relate to communication.

A few weeks prior to the rut, however, rubs begin showing up again. Many of them become rub lines and are effective for bowhunters. I have taken several bucks during the early archery season while sitting near rub lines, even though the rut was still several weeks away.

These rub lines continue to be effective up until, and during the rut. Several new rub lines also may show up during this same period. The bucks may change their bedding and feeding areas, which may alter their rub lines, but the possibilities of finding them are good if you continue to scout and watch for fresh sign. When the rut progresses and the bucks expand their search for estrous does, so will the rub lines. I have enjoyed more success, though, hunting rub lines before the rut. During the rut the bucks travel more often and appear to be inconsistent. For me, prime time is about two weeks before the peak of the rutting season.

I especially like finding rub lines where bucks may bed in thick areas. These lines are often short, normally 200 yards or less. But they offer excellent opportunities to ambush an unsuspecting buck. You must be careful, though, not to push a buck out of its bedding area.

I pay special attention to rub lines that occur in the same areas each year. Many times I will find the same trees are rubbed, while other times there will be new trees hit nearby. I really enjoy finding scarred trees from a previous year, and watch them closely to see if the line reopens.

Normally, you can tell how fresh a rub is by the shredded bark underneath the tree, or by the color of the rubbed area. A bright, almost white rub will usually indicate it is fresh. However, the type of tree may affect the appearance of the rub. Although rubbing will polish the antlers white, several variations of antler color do exist. I must believe that the kind of tree that is rubbed will also affect the color of the antlers.

When I hunted in Alberta, Canada, for example, I did not see any bucks that had antlers as white as those in the Midwest. As a matter of fact, some could be considered walnut. This includes the hefty buck I took only two weeks prior to the peak of the rutting season. By the number of rubs I found in the area where I took the deer, there is no doubt the buck had been at it for quite some time. Yet, none of the bucks I saw in the area carried white antlers.

I also enjoy success hunting rub lines during the post-rut period. Normally, I begin locating new rub lines about two to three weeks after the peak. There are not as many when compared to the pre-rut, and they are not as easily located. By this time in many states, the firearm season has already taken a toll on the bucks in a given area. Simply said, there are fewer bucks remaining. But those that do open rub lines offer opportunities for the late archery season hunter and the muzzleloader enthusiast.

In Indiana, there is no hunting for six days. When the season reopens, however, after the close of the firearm season in Indiana, bowhunters and muzzleloading fans can start again. A few years ago, I used the 6-day period to locate a rub line that I had never seen in this particular area. It was about 1/4 mile from where I had previously hunted. The rub line extended for a distance of 300 yards. The trees ranged in diameter from 1 to 6 inches, and the shredded gouges left little doubt that a respectable buck had followed the rub line frequently.

It was somewhere around 8:30 a.m. on the first morning of the split season when I caught movement to my left. Seconds later, I spotted the big buck as it cautiously followed the rub line closer to my stand. As I readied myself for the shot, I tried to calm my nerves. It was hard to believe that it would happen so easily. The buck, a 10-pointer that just missed the Pope & Young minimum score, passed by less than 10 yards from my tree stand. When he quartered-away, I took the easy shot without hesitation.

Trails can usually be found along rub lines, but don't be discouraged if they are not weathered with usage. Seldom do these trails look like major highways. In many cases, only a particular buck and an occasional group of other deer may be using the trail. If the trail and rub line is a link to the food and bedding area, it will probably make an excellent ambush location.

Hunting fresh rub lines have become my most effective method for ambushing bucks. I will choose this over a scrape most any day. When a buck makes a habit of leaving a signpost at various locations, he is attempting to communicate. More than likely he will return to see if any other deer got the message.

CHAPTER 6

PRODUCTIVE
SCRAPE HUNTING

I have never met a deer hunter that did not become enthusiastic after discovering a fresh scrape. Regardless of its location, size or at what stage of the rut you find the scrape, it can start the candle burning. We are often immediately compelled to set up a stand or ground blind with the intent of intercepting a buck that has left his mark.

Unfortunately, few scrapes offer the potential for success. Perhaps that is why I included *productive* in the chapter title. I believe it is vitally important to determine whether a scrape will be visited again, and be there with all the patience you can muster. A scrape can cost you valuable hunting time, or it can turn a boring season into a very productive hunt. Simply said, you must locate an active scrape, and stay with it until it pays.

We have been hearing about boundary, secondary and primary scrapes for several years. You probably already know the definition of each. Boundary scrapes are those which appear

71

along the edges of fields or particular territorial locations. Most bucks scent mark their territory boundaries by making scrapes around a given area.

Secondary scrapes are those that usually appear away from the boundary borders, but are not nearly as large as primary scrapes. I cannot really say, however, that I know the difference in a primary and secondary scrape. I've located many scrapes about the size of a basketball backboard, and consider these to be primaries. But I am not so sure they have helped me anymore than smaller scrapes that many consider to be secondary scrapes. I consider any scrape located away from agricultural fields, regardless of its size, to have potential. Thus it could be called a primary. What really matters is the potential of a buck returning.

Caution should be used to prevent leaving human scent near a scrape.

I believe that any scrape found near a bedding area or along a rub line offer the deer hunter an excellent opportunity. There is a good chance this scrape will be visited again.

If you have kept an eye on a particular scrape, and have noticed more than one visitation, it will offer possibilities.

Many of these hot scrapes may appear near the bedding area of bucks, does or both, and along frequently used trails where rubs are present. I don't really care if the scrape is no more than a 2-foot circle. If a buck, or bucks have made a return call, then I probably will do the same.

Before discussing the hot scrapes any further, I would like to mention a couple of factors regarding boundary scrapes. They normally show up along the fringes during the rut, but sometimes they will be spotted prior to the deer season in the late summer or early fall shortly after the velvet is removed. Beyond any doubt, this occurs when the competition is high. The more bucks in a given area, the more boundary scrapes you will find during the pre-season period.

In most areas, I seldom find scrapes appearing until about three weeks prior to the peak of the rutting season. Sporadically, though, I have discovered isolated pockets where several scrapes are found in September in Indiana. These are normally the boundary scrapes I previously mentioned. Although they offer little chance when hunting over them, they do let you know that several bucks are using that particular area.

I can recall a pre-season scouting trip in the early 1980s where I located at least two dozen scrapes in a 200-yard radius. During the first 10 days of the early archery season I saw at least five different bucks. The trails did not appear better than those in other areas I had hunted, nor did there seem to be more deer. There was a higher concentration of bucks, however, which led to the numerous boundary scrapes and buck sightings.

HUNTING FARMLAND BUCKS

The mature bucks will do most of the scraping.

Most deer hunters know a scrape is a section of ground that has been pawed by a deer to remove the debris. Bucks and does will urinate in the pawed area, and bucks occasionally chew the overhanging limbs. The *preorbital glands* above the eyes are often rubbed by the deer to leave a scent mark.

I have always put more emphasis on scrapes that show evidence of chewed limbs, or limbs and trees nearby that have been thrashed by the antlers of a rutting buck. But I do not disregard scrapes if these signs are not present. The hottest scrape I have ever hunted seldom showed signs of rubbing nearby, and seldom were chewed limbs visible.

This scrape was impressive, though, simply because it was opened each year about one week before the peak of the rut. It was located near a bedding area in a 40-acre plot of thickets, about 150 yards from a consistent agricultural food source. I shot several bucks with bow and gun near the scrape in a period of six years. I have never taken a buck servicing the scrape, but that was because I did not give them the opportunity. Unfortunately, after logging occurred in the area, the scrape became history.

Some have claimed that scrape lines have the best potential for success. Personally, I seldom find enough scrapes in a given area with a pattern that resembles what I would consider a scrape line. A rub line is another story, as you have already read in the preceding chapter. I have found several scrapes in a given area, but I cannot usually call it a scrape line. I put far more emphasis on a single scrape that remains active each year. You can bet there is a darn good reason that a buck returns to the same scrape year after year.

As for several scrapes in a surrounding area, which some might consider to be a scrape line, I have never seen them all get hit again when the next rut arrived.

Locating the repeating scrapes will require footwork. You simply have to cover a lot of ground during the rutting season. It also will help to make notes of your whereabouts each time you locate a potentially good scrape. A topographic map will assist you in learning the area and selecting the possible bedding and feeding areas. You can back this up with a return visit the following season during the rut to determine if the scrape has been opened.

I seldom pay attention to tracks found in scrapes. Often, other deer will pass over them on a routine walk. I do pay attention, though, if droppings are found in scrapes. I have visited a scrape one day and saw no fresh sign. The following day I would return to find droppings, even though the scrape had not been freshly pawed. I believe the scrape may also have been urinated in whenever the droppings are present. This usually dries, however, before I make my return visit.

I am uncertain if all bucks participate in scraping, and I seriously doubt that the small bucks will practice this ritual on a regular basis. I have spent countless hours photographing white-tailed bucks, and when busy watching a respectable buck that is tending does, I usually notice them making scrapes regularly. Only occasionally do the small bucks that are nearby participate in making a scrape.

Many years ago, Drs. Larry Marchinton and Karl Miller studied several penned deer. The bucks ranged from 1 1/2 to 8 1/2-years-old. Surprisingly the mature bucks, those 3 1/2-years-old and older did most of the scraping.

Unfortunately, I cannot say that every buck I have taken near a scrape has been a mature buck. On the contrary, most have been youngsters—1 1/2-years-old. Bucks will not usually scrape on densely covered soil. If they have to paw away numerous vines or debris in order to make a scrape, they will pass the opportunity. Normally, they choose areas where only a few leaves need removing. A preference often includes a thin weedy section near a tree.

I also believe the type of tree will make a difference. Most bucks have their preferences, which can change with geographical locations. In the Midwest, pin oaks are favored far more than other oaks.

Almost always, they will chew the overhanging limbs when they make a scrape near the base of the pin oak. Dogwoods, though plentiful in most regions, are seldom selected. Maples often become a popular choice, as do some pines.

Patience is required to hunt a scrape successfully, but no amount of patience you can muster will help if you hunt a scrape that is not productive. If the scrape has been hit more than once in the same year, or has reappeared in consecutive years, your

Active scrapes are normally those that show evidence of limb chewing from above.

patience will increase your odds of taking a buck. But this may require hunting at times that you would normally prefer to be out of the woods. Midday is a prime time to catch bucks visiting a scrape. It is hard to hunt this time of day regularly if you are the normal 3-hour morning and evening hunter. I know, because I prefer to be there when the sun rises and sets. But when I think back to a few instances where I have taken bucks between the hours of 11 a.m. and 1 p.m., I gain enough confidence to head for the woods during the lunch hours.

The winter months, even though the scraping may have subsided, is the best time of year to locate scrapes you may have missed during the hunting season. They are on the ground to stay until the spring sprouts begin, and can easily be spotted.

A doe also will visit a scrape and scent the chewed limb.

You must also hunt the productive scrapes at the right times during the hunting season. The most active period for the scraping activity usually occurs about one week prior to the peak. My favorite time begins about two weeks before the peak, and up to one week after. The bucks are the most active during this period. *Testosterone* levels (caused by the lesser amount of sunlight that releases hormones) are the highest in bucks at this time. It is also the time the hunter should become active.

Timers are readily available to the deer hunter in many sporting goods stores or catalogs. They can be rigged to your scrape to let you know if and when a buck makes a return visit while you are away. However, a passing deer that makes no connection with the scrape can trip your timer and cause confusion.

Many hunters have compared hunting over scrapes to hunting over bear baits, but I see very little comparison. A bear is much more reliable with hitting a bait. They may not show up in the daylight hours, but they usually do return. Scrapes simply are not that dependable. As an avid bear hunter, I would speculate that of half the baits that are hit, about half of the bears return. As for a buck that has visited a scrape, I would say about 20 percent make a return visit. I am judging that by scrapes that I have watched consistently during the rut. The size of the area a buck covers when making scrapes will vary. Although most will stay in a one or two mile radius, studies have shown some to travel up to 10 miles. I believe, though, that a buck has certain areas in which to scrape. This does not signify a preferred breeding location, however. They will breed wherever and

When a buck finds an estrous doe, he is ready to breed regardless of the locality.

whenever they locate an estrous doe. Keep in mind, if a doe is ready she will also be anxious to breed. This often occurs during the buck's active period, which may bring the doe to an active scrape.

Mock scrapes are sometimes produced by hunters to entice a buck. Although I have not experienced success with synthetic scrapes, others say they do work. On a couple of occasions I have had mock scrapes hit, but never has my patience been strong enough to keep me there long enough to see if the buck would return.

I would recommend wearing rubber boots if you make a mock scrape. You should anyway to reduce the amount of human scent, regardless of whether you are hunting a man-made or natural scrape. A buck will surely have his nose on the ground when he visits the scrape, and one mistake can cost you.

Whenever a rain shower has passed, I make it a point to hunt near a scrape. This is prime time for a buck to revisit the scrape, simply because he wants to freshen it. I can't say that he is thinking along these lines, but I do know that scrapes are frequently hit within 24 hours of being washed out.

When hunting bucks, scrapes are my least effective method. Normally, I am more successful when hunting rubs, bedding areas and food sources. But I have taken a few bucks over scrapes, and I will continue hunting them for years to come. That is providing I can get the jump on productive scrapes. In my opinion, it's a matter of finding those that will receive a return visit, and having the patience to wait for a potential customer.

CHAPTER 7

CALLS AND SCENTS

The use of calls and scents has grown in popularity during the last decade. The industry now offers about every imaginable product, and has contributed to the success of many deer hunters. Some hunters, though, remain skeptical about the usefulness of many products.

I have had the opportunity to field test several products while hunting with bow and gun. Some have produced results, while others failed when conditions appeared perfect. However, I have learned that the hunter must use calls and/or scents at the right times, and have a good understanding of their intended function.

I don't know of any products that work on any buck at any time during the hunting season. Each buck appears to have its own personality, and seldom will two respond the same. The idea is to grab a buck's interest, and have them respond by coming into range. Any condition, or mood the buck possesses, will affect their response. What one likes, another may not. And if a particular buck doesn't respond one day, the possibility exists that he will respond on another. It's that simple. The whitetail relies on its senses to communicate and socialize with other deer. Their sense of smell may inform them *who* has been there, and their hearing may tell them what is going on in the nearby thicket. The hunter must create a diversion, or signal enough curiosity to lure a buck into range. Unfortunately, the hunter may have to purchase several products to accomplish this task. Calls and scents are not cheap, and it may cost a few dollars to experiment. But there is potential in farmland country because of the number of whitetail deer, and excessive traveling routes. These factors set the stage for using many products.

CALLS

In 1980, Larry W. Richardson and his colleagues recorded the sounds of about forty bucks and does at Mississippi State University. In their recording, *The Acoustics of Whitetail Deer*, they distinguished eight stereotypic sounds of which the grunt and bleat became the most important to the deer hunter. Both can be used to signal a mating urge or contact call when the proper conditions or sound exist.

The grunt produces a deep "urp" sound. This call works well prior to the rut, as well as during and after the peak breeding period. The grunt represents a "tending" call, and may attract any antlered buck. This does not necessarily mean, however, that all bucks will respond to a given grunt.

When a buck hears a grunt, he accepts it as a communicative desire for a doe. To him it means another buck is aggressively pointing out the chance of an estrous doe's presence. I have watched several bucks grunt while they were in hot pursuit of a doe, or grunt as they attempted to locate a doe that has left a cold trail. How often they grunt may depend on how

Both the grunt and bleat call will attract a buck when used at the proper times.

excited they become, or the nature of their mood. Strangely enough, I have watched some bucks pass by that grunted with each step they took, even when there were no does in the immediate area, or any that had passed through. I speculate these bucks are simply thinking about the possibility of finding an estrous doe.

Many have claimed that an older buck will produce a deeper grunt. I am not so sure, though, that there is substantial proof to back this statement. I have heard countless bucks grunting, particularly while photographing them during the rut, and have had a difficult time trying to determine the mature bucks from the young fellers. Some do sound different, but the courser sounds do not always reflect on a mature buck. Many grunt calls, however, do vary with sound and tone. And I have spooked a few bucks here and there when testing the products. More about that in a moment.

The loudness of the grunt, whether it comes from the real thing or another hunter, depends on closeness and wind. On a calm day I have heard bucks grunt at 100 yards, but usually they are heard at 75 yards or less. Sometimes I have no idea if a buck is in the area—until I hear the grunts. On a breezy day, however, you may not hear a grunting buck within 50 yards.

The bleat is considered a ''contact'' call. Deer of all sex and age use it throughout the year, but as is with the grunt, the pitch and tone will tell who is giving the call. Most of the earlier commercial deer calls were bleats or distress cries. These calls will attract deer, but their higher-pitched tones reflect those of fawns and do not always work well to attract bucks. Does, when bleating, give more of a medium or deep-pitched *buaaaaa,* which lasts about one-half second or less.

Doe bleats offer several advantages to the hunter. Bucks hear doe bleats throughout the year. When a buck hears this during the rut, he is going to be enticed if he has any desire at all to find a doe. In addition, a doe bleat never frightens bucks. Although I have seen small bucks sneak away when I grunted with too much authority, I have never frightened a buck by bleating. Even if a buck does not respond positively to my doe bleat, at least I haven't sent him running from my ambush location.

Although I have taken several bucks using the bleating sound, I remember my first incident well. A buck, which I considered to be a possible Pope & Young candidate, walked by me at a distance of about 50 yards. My first bleat stopped him, and he started toward me after the second. Walking deliberately,

The doe bleat is common communication, and is heard during all seasons of the year.

he did not stop until he was only twenty yards from the base of my tree. Fortunately, for him, a small maple covered his vitals and I lost the opportunity of a lifetime. So close, and yet so far.

Later that season, I killed a smaller, five-point buck after offering him three bleats. My son, upon seeing and hearing the results, used the bleat during the firearm season to call a buck into easy slug range. Since then, we have both used the bleat with excellent results.

Although the bleat is basically a contact call, keep in mind that an estrous doe will use this sound in an attempt to bring a buck to her. This will work for the hunter in the same way.

Calls, either grunts or bleats, can be used to attract a buck passing by out of range, or in an attempt to bring in a buck you did not know existed.

When I call to a buck passing by, I start with a soft call, and increase the volume as necessary. Many calls are manufactured to be loud, while others can only be increased by blowing harder.

If a buck does not stop when I call, I assume it has not heard the grunt or bleat. I then increase the volume until I know I have the buck's attention. When a walking buck suddenly stops and throws their head in my direction, I can assume he heard the call. I should add, I do not grunt repeatedly. When I try to stop a buck, I grunt or bleat once or twice. Once I have his attention, I may call again to let him know my location. Be assured, though, if a buck is extremely close the call may spook him. He knows exactly where the call came from, and expects to see or smell the communicating deer. The thickness and visibility should affect your decision to call when a buck is close.

I have used the calls on several occasions in an attempt to draw in a buck that I did know was there. Many times this occurs when I am ready to leave my stand, just to see what is around. Occasionally, it does work.

One year before starting this book, I used the grunt to lure in a buck in the final minutes of my morning hunt. I had not seen any deer, and I had to leave my stand early to attend an appointment. I gave two soft grunts. After five minutes and getting no response, I called again with more intensity. I heard the buck approaching before I could clearly shoulder the muzzleloader. The 5-pointer walked past me at 25 yards, looking for the buck he had heard, but did not get the opportunity to inspect the surrounding area.

The distress calls of the fawn has also grown in popularity. They will attract any deer on the right day, including the

Geary Crutsinger tries the grunt call to see if he can lure a buck into shooting range.

HUNTING FARMLAND BUCKS

Jim Hole of Edmonton, Alberta attempts to rattle up a buck.

bucks. Several hunting videos demonstrate the potential of this useful call, and I would suggest that anyone watch them to see their effectiveness.

The distress calls often work when other calls fail. When you use the grunt or bleat in an attempt to attract a buck that is accompanied by does, you will often be rejected. The distress calls, though, may bring a group of deer (bucks included) right into your honey hole.

Rattling antlers offer another approach for attracting bucks, but the effectiveness of this technique often depends on several factors, including the created sounds and the number of bucks in a given area.

First let's review technique. There is far more to rattling than clanging antlers together and sitting back to wait for a shot. Bucks either spar or fight, and it's important to understand the distinction.

Sparring is basically a social activity. Younger bucks spar, and most matches remain friendly. Sparring takes place long before the rut gets in gear and lasts until bucks shed their antlers. Even then, without antlers, younger bucks will still push and shove on occasion to establish the pecking order. Buck

The author shot this Pope & Young buck at 18 yards. The huge deer walked within bow range after 10 minutes of rattling.

fights, serious clashes of antlers, generally occur among more dominant bucks during the peak of the rut. When two bucks cannot resolve their rank by physical posturing, all-out battles ensue, sometimes to the death.

Both sparring matches and serious fight sequences can be reproduced to attract bucks. The difference lies in the size of the bucks that will respond. If you only want a buck of trophy potential, then the hard-nosed fight may come closer to getting the job done. On the other hand, sparring matches will draw in bucks of all sizes.

In most areas, the bulk of the harvest consists of yearling deer. And if there is a mature buck nearby, he must be within hearing distance and not already preoccupied with available

An all-out buck fight may frighten a young buck.

does. Most experienced rattlers will not start with the *real* fighting, simply because it will frighten less dominant bucks, who may very well be the only deer in the area. Sparring, on the other hand, may attract any buck, including the real monster himself.

Like many others, I did not rattle often in the past because of my lack of confidence in the technique. I thought of it as a method that only worked in Texas, but I was wrong. In 1990, I hunted in Alberta with Jim Hole of Classic Outfitters. After Jim's demonstration of sparring and fighting, it became obvious why I had not been successful in the past.

Jim always begins with a sparring match keeping the antlers against his legs to create a heavier and more genuine pushing sound, while lightly tinkling the tips together. He switches to louder, down-to-earth fights only when sparring fails to attract attention.

With the rut still two weeks away I gave the method a try. On my third rattling sequence a huge buck came in to 18 yards and my arrow flew true.

If you don't have a set of real antlers for rattling, several companies offer synthetic antlers that sound like the real thing. They can be used for both fighting and sparring.

The buck-to-doe ratio is very important. Rattling in areas that support several bucks is sure to increase your chances. In areas where there are 6 to 7 does for each buck, there is less chance of attracting a buck's attention.

SCENTS

Making sense out of scents may require more education than many of us have. The market is currently flooded with brand names and types of scents, and we have to scratch our heads to come up with something that we think will work.

Several types of scents are available, but cover-ups and sex lures remain the most popular. Cover-up scents are offered to mask human odors, while the sex scents are made to lure a buck into making a big mistake. Masking scents vary considerably, from sweet smells to apples, acorns, pine, cedar, sage, earth or predator scents. I am sure that sentence did not cover everything available, but it does get the point across. You can find something that fits your needs, and hope it works.

The sex lures include urines and estrous doe scents. Many claim they come from the real thing, while others are made with synthetic products. I don't believe one is better than the other. If a synthetic scent is made as a replica of the *Real McCoy*, it would appear to have the same chance of working.

Like many deer hunters, I have used all types of scents the past few years. A few worked to attract deer or cover up my human scent, but others failed when it seemed they should have worked. Regardless of the outcome, we should understand that whitetails rely primarily on their sense of smell to survive.

Buck lures entice many hunters simply because of their title. Many of us have gotten the idea that we only have to spray a little on a nearby bush and get ready. Nothing is further from the truth. First of all, a buck has to pass by close enough to smell it, and then have enough interest to follow it in for a closer investigation.

Many hunters claim to have excellent results with doe-in- heat lures and other sex related scents. These scents, usually intended to dispense a doe-in-estrous odor, would seemingly cause a rutting buck to come a runnin'. But some hunters, however, think sex scents do far more good in mock or genuine scrapes.

Most lure companies recommend placing the scent canister a few feet off the ground to dispense it properly. Just

This hunter is applying cover-up scent.

how far a deer can detect the odor remains unknown. However, humidity and wind play a role, and often cause failures.

Professor Larry Marchinton and Karl Miller handle the white-tailed deer research at the University of Georgia. Marchinton said they have studied biological scent communications for years, and the subject is extremely complicated. Urine acquired from bucks and does has become popular with scent companies and hunters. Many think that urine used in a scrape produces the best results. Marchinton pointed out, however, that the signpost communication on the scrape and above it is complex.

"The forehead scent is important when rubbing trees and the branches above scrapes," Marchinton said. "In addition, the *preorbital* gland and saliva where they lick is meaningful to bucks. The dominant bucks not only do this above the scrapes, but they also appear to do most of the urinating on the scrape.''

Marchinton also said does seem more interested in the scrape itself, whereas bucks, young and old, showed more interest on the scents above.

The *tarsal* gland, located on the hind legs of the whitetail, allows deer to recognize each other. A few companies now use tarsal-gland scent as a lure, claiming deer want to investigate newcomers to the area.

I used the tarsal gland scent while hunting in northern Missouri a couple of years ago when hunting with a muzzleloader. I had forgotten about the scent until an 8-pointer focused his attention on it long enough for me to squeeze off a shot at close range.

The success of scents often depends on how the hunter dispenses them. Some companies make a boot pad to handle the operation. An elastic strap fits over the boot to hold the pad in place. Many hunters use the pad and scent when they walk to their stand. One question, however, is whether a deer would back-trail the scent. No doubt, the scent on the pad weakens as the trail continues, and if a buck detects the trail he would likely follow it away from the hunter.

One remedy, which I have tried, reverses the method. The hunter puts the scent on at the stand, walks away, and then removes the pad and returns to the stand. Thus the trail grows stronger as the buck follows it to the hunter. This is providing the deer does not pick up the scent the hunter left when walking back to the stand.

Other dispensers include wicks in tubes, and battery-powered fans to blow the scent into the area.

Cold weather will affect scents and, if temperatures drop low enough, freeze them. A few companies have designed heated containers. These battery-operated devices will heat the canister and allow the scent to dispense through an open vent.

Cover scents have worked better for me than most sex scents, but I have found it often requires using a bundle to mask my odor. Let's face it: We stink, at least in the deer's opinion. Our skin produces bacteria that produce odors. Even though we can't detect our scent, deer can easily smell us at distances up to 100 yards when conditions are right. Both cleanliness and the foods you eat affect the amount of odor you produce.

Hunters often use animal scents to mask themselves or their travel routes. Fox urine has been widely used in recent years. Those looking for something different, might want to try squirrel or rabbit scents.

I believe in a few calls and scents. Many however, have not worked. This leads me to believe some poor products exist. On the other hand, every company claims success with their product. Perhaps the best method is to try as many as you can afford to see what works. Remember that nothing works all the time, even though a few companies claim they do. At least one thing remains a fact, however: The whitetail will always depend on sound and scent for communication.

This buck is following the trail of a receptive doe that just passed through. If he loses her trail, he will remain persistent and keep searching to locate her before another buck services her.

CHAPTER 8

AMBUSH TECHNIQUES

The ambush method is no doubt the most popular technique used by deer hunters. The tree stand business has boomed for several years, and it is likely to continue. Stalking a whitetail buck is not an easy task, even when perfect conditions exist. There are a selected few, though, who have the special talent needed for successful stalking. I have taken a few whitetail bucks while hunting on the ground, but my preference is by way of the perch.

I have learned over the years, and so has every other tree stand hunter, that there is a lot to selecting the right locations. And there is even more to making it work. First, the right trail must be selected to get the opportunity at a buck. The hunter also must place their stand properly, and keep their presence hidden when and if the chance to shoot ever arrives. Last, it is necessary to plan the proper approach and departure when traveling to and from the stand, and not over-hunt the selected location.

I have taken several bucks while hunting what I refer to as buck trails. I am not trying to say that there are trails that only bucks use. On the contrary, does and fawns travel any trail at any location if it offers them access to where they want to go, or provides them with an easy route. But there are trails that bucks will use with more regularity than others. These can be referred to as buck trails.

A master trail can be identified in any area by its appearance and age. If you are familiar with an area and have hunted it for several years, you probably can recall a few trails that have been there longer than you can remember.

The master trail should be thought of as a highway. It is the main link between bedding and feeding areas, but only to some degree. The most important part of its identification lies in its length. They generally cover an area from field to field. Simply said, they will begin at an agricultural location, and end at another. They can be several hundred yards long, or a mile or more depending on the amount of forested habitat. The side trails that intercept the master trails may lead to bedding areas or a food source. These runways are often used by bucks.

Deer seldom travel the master trails very far, even though they are the longest trails in any area. Instead, they use many side trails to link with the master trails. They may leave a bedding area and use a side trail to pick up the master trail before turning onto another side trail.

Another reason the master trail is so easy to identify is because of its age, thus making it easy to see. The side trails that guide deer to bedding and feeding areas change from season to season, or year to year, thus being used only some of the time.

After I eliminate the master trails, I spend time walking the side trails. Many of these will be traveled frequently by the does and fawns, while a few will be traveled by the bucks, or in some cases, one buck only.

Active buck trails are those that usually connect to the master trails.

It is my preference, other than during the late seasons, to hunt those trails that lead into bedding areas and dense cover. So often, the thicker the area, the better chance that a buck will use it. This can usually be told by the sign that is found. When rub lines exist along a side trail leading to a thick area, you can count on a buck being close. And in some cases I have even jumped a buck from its bed. This also guarantees me that a buck uses the trail with some regularity. However, it may not help your future hunting. The big boys have a tendency to move to a different bedding area when this occurs, and the hunter must be careful that it doesn't happen.

During the archery hunting season in the early 1980s, I had walked a side trail for about 200 yards when I spooked a dandy buck from his bed. The rut was going strong, and I assumed the deer was probably gone forever. However, I returned a couple of days later and jumped the same buck from the same thicket. I assumed if it happened twice it might just happen again.

The following day I placed my stand within 100 yards of the bucks bedding area. I planned to use it the first day of the firearm season, which was less than 48 hours away.

Though opening morning came and went without seeing the buck, I returned the next morning to give it one more chance. The second day I was greeted with a cold, light drizzle, and it took all I had to stay in the tree. However, I was glad I did. The buck came slipping through two hours after I had been in my stand. One shot from the slug gun dropped the buck less than 50 yards from his bedding area. His rack had an inside spread of 15 inches, but carried only six points. I am still uncertain why the buck continued to use the bedding area after being run out on two occasions.

Perhaps my favorite method for locating buck trails is to hunt it and see what is there. There is probably nothing closer to the truth than the old saying, ''seeing is believing.'' If I suspect that the trail I've chosen has been used by bucks, I hang a stand and hunt it when wind conditions are favorable. And if after so many trips I do not see a buck, I move on to another area. Usually I pick several locations to hunt, and a switch does the area good. My concentration eventually focuses on the location where I have seen the most bucks.

I am convinced that bucks prefer to travel the same route, but this does not mean they will use only one for traveling to and from a bedding area. You can bet they have alternate trails that lead them to the same general vicinities. The hunter must locate the preferred routes, or spend enough time at the selected location to give the buck enough time to travel the route. The most important factor is to give up, though, when the bucks fail

Bucks like it thick.

to show themselves. We all enjoy seeing deer, even if they carry no head-gear. However, you must force yourself to concentrate on other possibilities if you hope to take a buck. The does and fawns can bring the bucks in during the rutting period, but I have had far more success going after bucks on their turf.

Keep in mind that any buck trail can change rapidly. The master trails always seem to look about the same, mainly because of their age. The side trails, though, will never appear to be heavily used, even when they are active. And they can suddenly become inactive. Changes in food sources, bedding areas and/or the rut can cause any trail to turn sour.

As mentioned previously, I prefer to hunt thick areas with both bow and gun. These areas are generally small and surrounded by standing timber. They usually grow up with high vegetation, such as honeysuckle, briars, saplings and low shrubs. Many areas that have been logged eventually will grow into dense-cover, usually about four to five years after they are timbered. These openings provide a great deal of food for all wildlife, and eventually good cover.

Hunters often overlook these ideal locations, simply because they are not appealing to the eye. They often avoid walking through them, and instead take the easy routes that surround the dense cover. However, they don't realize that by doing so they are missing out on a good opportunity to be close to the deer—especially the bucks.

When you see deer, you are likely to get action, simply because you are not apt to see them unless they are within shooting range. It is important to clear your shooting lanes, whether you are hunting the dense cover with bow or gun. I do not clear an area to the point that it looks cleared, however. A deer will often notice this, and avoid the area. If I am bowhunting, I will clear about three shooting lanes. Then, if a deer gets by one before I can shoot, I may get another chance. I hunt with the gun in the same locations where a bow is used. It is not necessary to clear, and the deer will be familiar and relaxed with the clearing you have already done.

The deer in thick cover almost always seem relaxed as they approach your location. There is usually browse, which will be to your advantage; it keeps the deer moving slowly. The thick cover that surrounds them will keep them feeling more secure and will increase your chances of seeing deer, even in late morning or early afternoon.

Deer runways are easily found in the thick areas. Deer can travel only certain routes, because of the heavy brush. It is a little like an obstacle course that forces them to move in and around the heavy brush. This is to your advantage, because they will most likely pass by you within shooting range.

One disadvantage to hunting dense thickets is trees—or a lack of them. You normally do not get a large selection to choose from, and hanging a portable, using a climber or building a permanent stand presents a problem. It becomes difficult at this time to hunt with the correct wind direction, because of little tree selection, and it is important to select your ambush location carefully. Many trees also may leave you silhouetted.

Deer may walk in the thickets more quietly than through a wooded area. There are fewer leaves to give you that *crunching* sound we all like to hear. But when the freezes start, you can hear their approach much more easily.

Hanging a stand in the right location is very important. A hunter can do everything right up to this point, and still blow

An ambush location should not be over-hunted.

it when truth day arrives.

I no longer build permanent stands. After the introduction of climbing and portable stands several years ago, I threw the hammer and nails aside. And now on many public areas, the building of stands is prohibited.

I only used climbing stands shortly after their introduction, and quickly switched to the portables when they became available. I prefer them because of their quietness and convenience. I can carry in a portable, use either screw-in or strap-on steps, and have the blind ready to hunt in a few minutes. When it comes time to leave, I can quietly depart.

Whenever a climbing stand was used, it seemed to catch on brush whenever I entered or departed the area. I now own several portable stands, which I conveniently hang in different areas for both my son and myself. Even now I often discover that more are needed. But they are expensive, and there is a risk of them being stolen.

I prefer to select several areas for many reasons. First, I don't like overhunting a location. Any area will dry up after continued use. Each time you visit your stand a disturbance is made. In addition, no matter what you have done to prevent leaving human scent, some odor will surely find its way to the surrounding vegetation as you pass through it to and from your stand.

The amount of pressure your area can take depends entirely on how often you hunt. I prefer to hunt a location only two or three times, even when the wind is in my favor. Although it can be difficult to stop using a stand when you are seeing deer, you must force yourself to go elsewhere occasionally. I have heard the stories of many who saw several deer each time they hunted a particular location, and then heard how the sightings dwindled. My personal experiences also have demonstrated that an area can burn out without prior warning.

Indiana muzzleloading hunter Jimmy Meyer hopes for a shooting opportunity if the wind remains favorable.

HUNTING FARMLAND BUCKS

Many hunters have preached that you can move too much. They say your best bet is to stick with one location. They claim this will guarantee you will be there at the right time. They base their theory upon a buck using a trail only now and then, and if you change locations you are sure to miss the action.

As far as I'm concerned, there is only one right time to hunt an area. Your attention must focus on the wind. The hunter must practice self control and restrain themselves from hunting a certain location when the wind is blowing from the stand to the deer. It is a hard thing to do, but it is vitally important. I have taken chances, and they always seem to catch up with me.

Many times I like switching to another area just for a change in scenery. This is probably a poor excuse for success, but it does help. I get tired of looking at the same trees, and tend to loose confidence when I visit the same area regularly. After changing locations, I become more enthusiastic. I spend less time day-dreaming and more time goes into the hunt.

Selecting several areas also will keep you from betting all your marbles on one location. I have found many areas that I just knew would pay off. Many did, but several have not. And after I have given a stand a fair chance, I remove it and place it elsewhere. I have always felt that it is never too late. I have moved stands for a one-day hunt, even if it was the last day of the season.

Without fail, the first time I hunt a stand is usually the best. When I look back at my records, I have taken almost 50 percent of the bucks harvested from stands that were hunted the first time. Even more impressive is the number of bucks that have been seen the first time I hunt the stand.

Everyone seems to prefer to hang a stand to suit their personal desires. Some hunters like facing into the area they expect the deer to come from, while others prefer to keep their back to the deer. My preference is to face into an approaching

Hunting pressure should affect the height of the tree stand.

buck so that I can closely watch every move it makes. I also assume that the buck will not see me first.

I hang my stand so that it will allow me to draw my bow or raise my gun without having to turn completely around. Since I am a right-handed shooter, I place my stand on the right side of the trail when looking toward the area the buck should come from. Of course, any deer hunter knows this can backfire. A buck is totally unpredictable and can come from the opposite direction you suspect, or pass by you on the side you did not suspect.

How high should you place your stand? This is also a matter of preference, but hunting pressure plays a big role in this.

The more hunting pressure that exists, the higher the stand should be.

I am not sure how much thinking ability the whitetail has, but I have seen the same deer that spotted me previously look up in an attempt to spot me again. Some biologists have claimed that a deer does not really think. Instead, they claim it reacts instinctively. I assume that any deer that has experienced prior hunter sightings from above will instinctively be provoked to look up. However, it is my belief that the whitetail can think and reason to some extent.

I know of one bowhunter who prefers to climb only about 10 feet. He never uses a tree stand, and relies instead on natural limbs to support him. Any hunter knows it can be difficult trying to shoot while standing on a limb, not to mention a little dangerous. But this hunter straps himself to the tree for security, and is very successful using this technique. He has taken several Pope & Young bucks, and claims he has rarely been spotted.

My preferred height is about 15 feet. I do not like sitting in the clouds, and getting higher always makes me feel a little uneasy. And if I am uncomfortable, it will affect my hunting and shooting.

The bowhunter's shot angle is also affected by the height of their tree stand. The higher you get, the sharper your angle. And when a buck is extremely close, it can cause your arrow to enter at a much sharper angle, thus missing one lung.

I seldom do anything different when hunting with a firearm. My stands are placed similarly. The only exception is visibility. If I want to cover a wider area, the stand will be placed where this is possible.

In the south, many hunters use the wooden box-type blinds. They are usually constructed on the edges of fields, and built for convenience. Most of them have small window openings surrounding them to allow you to shoot in any direction. I have used them in both Kentucky and Alabama during the firearm season, and have enjoyed the convenience they offer. In my neck of the woods, though, they will not work. The bucks seldom get to the fields during daylights hours, due to the number of roads and easy access into the agricultural areas.

Camouflage is vitally important when hunting any ambush location, whether it be a ground blind or tree stand. The main objective is to wear camo that will help you to blend and break up your outline. When hunting from a tree stand, though, I do believe it is possible to be spotted easier by an approaching buck when positioned at the skyline level. If trees or vegetation

An approaching doe can spoil your hunt for a buck if you do not blend with the background.

is not on all sides, you can easily be picked out. For this reason, I prefer to select areas along the sides of hills or near hollows. Sometimes, though, even in thickets where few trees are found, I'm forced to select unfavorable locations.

When I hunt at the skyline level, I will wear light colored camo to help me blend. The darker camo will cause you to stand out, and should be restricted to using on the ground, or whenever cover surrounds your tree stand.

Ultra-violet light has been discussed considerably in recent years. Some have doubted it, but I am convinced it can cause you trouble. Camo with UV brighteners will be noticed at dawn or dusk, and the hunter should consider using a UV killer to prevent this from occurring.

When bowhunting, I believe in placing my stand close to the trails. It does not bother me to hunt on top of the trail. There is nothing more frustrating than to watch a trophy buck walk by just out of range, but it often happens regardless of what you do to prevent it.

Choosing a ground blind location should be carefully thought out for both the gun and bowhunter. From a ground blind, you must be concerned with many factors. The visibility is poorer, and movements are generally restricted. The wind direction should always be considered, but it seems even more important when hunting from the ground.

I have used camo netting, but I prefer to make a ground blind from the natural surroundings. I gather enough debris to enclose me, and I use a small seat to keep me low and comfortable. Normally, I will shoot from the sitting position. The biggest problem with hunting the ground blind is a change in wind direction. In the Midwest we consistently have changes. The wind can be perfect when you arrive at your blind, but take a complete switch before the morning or evening hunt comes to a close. When hunting with a gun it may or may not matter, but during the archery season you are destined to roll with the punches.

There is another thing worth mentioning about ground blinds. Immediately after you break several limbs and clear a brushy area when constructing the blind, it pays to be ready. On numerous occasions I have had bucks walk in before I was ready.

Bucks are attracted to these sounds, and even tree stand hunters should be ready when clearing shooting lanes. I assume they may think a buck fight is in progress, or they are just curious to see what is causing the commotion.

I can still recall December 31, 1990. It was the last day of the Hoosier archery season and I had decided to assemble a ground blind about three hours before dark. I selected a pin oak tree to sit against, and had spent about 10 minutes breaking many lower, dead limbs. Just after completing the blind, I reached in my pocket to get my shooting tab. I was interrupted, however, by the sounds of an approaching deer behind me. I couldn't believe it when I spotted the monster buck standing less than 30 yards away, curiously looking over the area to see what had caused the disturbance. I could easily count five long points, including the brow tine on the right antler. There was no doubt it was the buck I wanted, but with my bow laying on the ground I had no chance to move. And as luck would have it, the buck became distracted by the sounds of barking dogs. Within seconds the huge deer turned and walked back from where he had come.

Your approach and departure is a major factor each time you visit your stand. I firmly believe these actions should be thought out prior to your hunt. You must plan your walk accordingly to keep any buck from knowing you have moved in on his turf.

Every hunter knows that each time we walk through an area, we leave some human scent. We know we should wear

Your approach and departure must be well-planned. Once a buck learns of your presence, he may move to another area.

rubber boots, as this reduces the risk of our scent being left where we walked. I agree with this tradition, but I am not so sure it is enough to let deer approach a stand as often as we would like. Sure, most everyone sees deer when we spend several hours in a blind. You can be positioned in a poor location, but as long as deer are in the area, eventually you will see something meander by. On the other hand, few of us realize the real potential some stand locations have. It could be that we might have seen deer twice as often if we handled our approach to the stand differently. Assuming you have taken the responsibility to minimize your scent, there are still a few other factors that I regard as even more important.

A hunter does not sound like a deer when they walk normally. The deer's walking pattern is much smoother than that of a man, partially because the deer is four-legged. The difference can be detected by another deer. This is going to be true whether or not an area has been hunted hard. If the conditions are right, it is not likely that a whitetail will confuse the sounds of a walking man with that of any other animal. When I say conditions, I am talking about ground cover and weather, both of which greatly determine how far and how well sound will carry. When wet and windy conditions prevail, it is possible you could reach your stand without any major disturbances, but this cannot be relied upon as an excuse to make the wrong approach.

Many hunters have perfected a walk that sounds almost like a deer. You can do this by walking on the tips of your toes, keeping the heels of your boots off the ground. If you study the sounds of a walking deer, you can use this method with excellent results. However, a dangerous situation might develop should another hunter mistake your walking pattern for that of a deer.

Although altering our walking gait will help, I believe it is even more important to plan the direction of your approach. Planning your approach does not mean taking the easiest and quickest route. It is planning a route by the way you are least likely to be noticed.

Let's face it; we are living in a lazy man's world. Everything is being made easier and faster for our satisfaction. We all like it that way and somehow, even with deer hunting, we are gifted with the same effort-saving products. When many hunters approach their stand, they pick the easiest route to get there, simply out of habit. But the end result is likely to be costing you deer.

When selecting a morning or evening ambush, start by walking the edge of the feeding areas. Consider the agricultural field as a river. The deer trails that adjoin the field are like the creeks that pour into the river, and this is where the deer come from. By walking these trails for a short distance and paying attention to the tracks, you will discover the direction the deer travel. If the majority of tracks lead toward the field, this trail is a good evening choice. If the tracks are leading away from the field and into dense cover, this will be a good morning selection since the trail is obviously leading to a bedding area. Of course, some trails will be master routes which show tracks leading in both directions.

Once you have located the choice trails and know when you will be hunting them, think about your entry and departure from the stand before selecting the exact point of your ambush. If you have walked your area thoroughly, you will be aware of the major bedding areas as well.

When planning your morning approach, you should base your decision on your proximity to the feeding area. Most hunters will arrive in their stands before first light. As this is usually a quiet time of morning when sound will carry the greatest, plan your approach from the farthest point possible from the feeding area. Deer still in the feeding area should not hear your approach.

When selecting the approach for the evening-only stand, try to choose a route closer to the feeding area. If too close to the bedding area, your approach may be heard and prevent the deer from using the trail when the time comes to move. However, a stand placed too close to the field may prove disastrous, as the deer may not reach you until after dark.

You must avoid walking through an agricultural food source in your approach to a morning stand, and when you leave your stand following the evening hunt.

Many hunters will place their stands close to the agricultural fields. This is true of morning or evening hunting. These are areas where you must avoid the field in your approach. I constantly see hunters who will walk the fields with their flashlights on to approach a stand in the pre-dawn hours. But deer that have just moved out of the fields into nearby timber and thickets are also spooked by the hunter moving through, particularly on the quiet mornings.

It is important that your morning approach does not take you between the feeding area and the stand. This is the key to a good morning hunt. Park your vehicle in a spot on the opposite side of your stand, away from the feeding area. Walk to your stand from that point, even if it means walking farther and going through rougher terrain.

Many times, this approach requires a few trips before a clear entrance can be made, but if you have become familiar with the area, you will soon become accustomed to the route, keeping you from straying or becoming lost. Clearing in some areas may be necessary, and marking the path with reflective tape also will help. Keep your approach as short as possible, but do not go between the feeding area and the stand.

Upon leaving in the late morning, plan to make a longer walk. You can assume deer have moved past your stand position to their bedding area, whether you saw them or not. When you leave your stand, go directly toward the feeding area and take a quick route back to the vehicle.

If using the same stand for both morning and evening hunts, use the same route with your evening approach that you used for your morning departure and vice versa. When hunting an evening stand only, plan your approach from the field and your departure through the bedding areas—the opposite of the morning plan. The deer have not yet traveled along the path of your approach, and should be gone from your departure route when you get there. These methods will give you the shortest routes in the dark hours and the longer routes in the daylight hours, which is to your advantage.

I usually avoid walking deer trails, but on occasion I have used them for short distances because they offer a quiet access. I have also noticed that deer will often use my trails.

A few years ago I cleared a trail through bramble bushes and small saplings for a distance of about 200 yards.

The trail allowed me to make a quiet approach or departure whenever necessary. Since the trail led to a food source, the deer soon began using it too. The following year I found myself hanging a portable stand along my cleared route because of an existing rub line that appeared promising.

It is not all the hours spent in the blind that causes the hunting to go sour, but the trips in and out each time you visit the same location. Regardless of how well you plan your approach, how quiet you are or how little scent you left, there is always some disturbance made. Eventually, it will catch up to you no matter what you do to prevent it.

There is no way you can always approach from downwind without eventually running into deer. Although the wind may be dominant from one direction most of the time, it is not constant. Eventually, it is going to change directions, making you go through the bedding area in the evening or the feeding area in the morning. At that point, you are going to have the deer moving out and away from your stand.

I sincerely believe the approach may determine the outcome of your hunt. Perhaps that is why I have discussed it so vigorously in this chapter.

HUNTING FARMLAND BUCKS

The author took this dandy 10-pointer during Indiana's late archery season, two weeks after the peak rutting period. A careful approach was planned to avoid leaving scent near the buck's trail.

CHAPTER 9

THE COLD FRONTS

Throughout this book I have discussed several effective, yet different methods for hunting farmland bucks. They have included the rut, food sources, funnels and a variety of other techniques. All the methods are somewhat similar; they consist of your ability to outsmart a buck while he functions normally. Simply said, a buck is a creature of habit. If you can accurately guess where they will spend time in the hours ahead, your chances of success increase tremendously.

This chapter, however, is about hunting bucks when the north wind blows. It does not mean you have to apply all the secret strategy you have learned, nor does it mean you need to plan a secret ambush in a forgotten thicket. If you can tolerate the weather and put in the necessary time, you stand a good chance of seeing a buck. The truth is, the bucks turn it on whenever the weather turns sour. During the rut a cold front is like a trigger to the reproductive system. Even during the pre-rut period a cold front can and will send a spark into a buck's imagination.

They say that experience is your best teacher. And when it comes to hunting cold fronts, that is how you will gain confidence that your hard hunting can pay off.

My first experience with hunting a cold front occurred several years ago. On that afternoon I was merely putting in my time. The temperature was around 36 degrees Fahrenheit and slowly falling. The north wind consistently blew about 15 to 20 miles per-hour, and a cold drizzle had settled in for the evening. But it was a chance to hunt, and so I chose a stand not far from a road, should I decide to come out early. The location of my stand had led me to believe that there was little or no chance of a buck passing by. And considering I had hunted it at least a dozen times without seeing a buck during the early archery season, it appeared I was in for a long afternoon.

As expected, the first hour went slow. I had begun to shiver and my damp body had taken all the punishment it could withstand when I caught movement to my left. Instantly, I saw the small rack the buck carried. From a sitting position I shouldered the slug gun to steady my aim. I squeezed off the shot and the 5-pointer ran less than 20 yards, piling up in the middle of a log jam.

Within minutes I had the buck field-dressed and began my short walk to the vehicle. At that moment I had considered the incident an error of nature. I felt it was simply a lucky moment for me, and an unlucky day for the buck, and assumed it probably would never happen again. However, just before reaching the vehicle a doe darted across the road. Seconds later a buck sped across in hot pursuit. Neither deer knew I was there, even though they crossed less than 40 yards from where I stood.

Still not convinced that the cold front had anything to do with affecting the buck's movements on that afternoon, I

Several deer used this trail when the cold front passed through.

returned a few days later with my dad. He still had a firearm tag to fill, and I planned to provide help if needed. At the time I did not think any help would be necessary because another approaching cold front had begun moving in just hours before we arrived. It was a similar evening, but the wind might have been a bit stronger. Like me, dad argued with himself for thinking about hunting on that kind of a day. However, his dedication to deer hunting overruled and he was in the stand by 3:30 p.m., giving him about 1 1/2 hours of daylight to hunt.

A short time later he was back at the vehicle telling me the story of how two bucks chased a doe past his stand on several occasions. After waiting for the right opportunity, he finally settled for the smaller of the two bucks. Not bad, considering it was an 8-pointer with a 16-inch inside spread.

HUNTING FARMLAND BUCKS

Bucks that have seemingly, disappeared may be compelled to move when a cold front blows in.

It was at this time I started believing in cold fronts, and less in Lady Luck. Prior to then, I had been convinced that perfect weather provided the best opportunities to take a buck. Now don't get me wrong. I still enjoy hunting a cool morning or evening when not even a leaf moves. Calm days are a favorite for most hunters. Let's face it. We can hear much better than we do on a breezy day, and our sixth sense seems to tell us that something good will surely happen.

Since that time, though, I have seen it proven over and over; buck movement does not occur simply because the weather is perfect for the hunter. There is generally a fair amount of whitetail movement when the weather is good, particularly with does and fawns. A deer's sense of smell is far more useful when there is no wind, and like you it also can hear better. A buck, however, is sparked by an oncoming cold front and is willing to take chances for the sole possibility of finding a doe.

Several years ago I kept an inventory on buck movement while hunting an area of about 500 acres. This stretch of ground was about 60 percent woods and thickets, and the rest agricultural. Since five of us leased the ground, it enabled me to keep records of all deer sightings from the beginning of the archery season, through the gun season, and up until the completion of the late bowhunting season. Data was also kept on weather, including temperatures, humidity, rainfall and wind speeds.

Overall, the final results showed more deer were seen on the pretty days when temperatures were cool and winds were calm. However, buck movement was stronger on certain bad days when the bucks were nearing, or had reached, the peak of the rut.

Hunting pressure, for the most part, was weaker during this period. I have never considered myself a fair-weather hunter, nor do I consider those that participated in the research to be. Many of these days, though, included heavy downpours, and little or no hunting was involved. Although that is common in the fall months in the Midwest, few hunters get used to the idea of sitting in a soaking rain. But when you take into consideration that fewer hunters hunted on the bad days, and yet more bucks were seen than on the perfect days, you begin to get a clearer picture.

Any deer hunter can verify that there is a far better chance of seeing bucks when the rut is going strong. This is no big news. But our results did show that several more bucks were seen when the weather was bad, with certain existing conditions in particular. We saw fewer bucks on the nice days, during the same period, even though the rut was in full swing.

Normally, the deer do not move on warm, breezy days. But when the wind switches to the north, the does and bucks may frequently travel in daylight hours.

I'm not trying to say that every time the weather is bad you are going to have the bucks up and moving. But the days when we had cold fronts moving in, even though the cold winds were blowing, we experienced the strongest buck movement.

There was little rain or snow involved, and the real key appeared to be the change of temperature, usually when a drop of 15 degrees or more had occurred. The wind would gust considerably during these periods, and the skies were always cloudy. Whenever downpours existed, or when the pressure system settled in, the buck activity declined.

Obviously, the bucks do not mind moving about on these days, even though the effectiveness of their vital senses are reduced. I am sure you have witnessed deer moving on windy days, and have seen them alerted by every pop and crack that can be heard.

Windy weather, from an incoming warm front, seems to play the opposite role with bucks. For that matter, it affects does and fawns, too. Our records indicated very few deer moved at these times. In some cases where warm fronts came in and sat on us, we went for several days without seeing any deer.

The bucks, on the other hand, must be seeing things differently on days when the cold fronts are moving in. I believe the fronts increase their urge to find the does. We know that the diminishing light of fall triggers the rut (a process called *photoperiodism*). Biologists have proven this over and over. However, cold weather has also been attributed somewhat in hastening the onset of strong rutting behavior, while a warm front seems to dampen a buck's sexual activity. When another cold front starts blowing in, a new spark is lit. The buck becomes anxious and prompted to move, and the hunter who happens to be in the right spot on the right day is rewarded.

I have also noticed a considerable increase in scrape activity during these periods. I have witnessed cold fronts come through during the night and have returned to an area I hunt the following morning to find new scrapes along the same trails that had none the evening before.

Another experience which sticks in my mind occurred while I was hunting with the smokepole, just after the regular firearm season had closed.

I had left work early in hope of being in my stand at least three hours before dark. But while driving the 10-mile stretch to my area, I spotted a small buck on the back of a harvested cornfield. The buck was in pursuit of a doe that was not about to oblige him. Since I had failed to take a buck thus far, I decided to try a stalk using a line of thickets to hide my approach. The weather was exactly as I described previously: dark, dreary, and

The stalker should be in the field on cold, windy days. This buck, prompted to move by the incoming front, looks for does in an open field.

windy. A light rain was just beginning to fall, which also would help me stalk the 200 yards that I needed to cover.

When I felt I had gone the needed distance, I eased out of the thickets, hoping the buck would be standing within black-powder range. However, he had apparently chased the doe further down the field, keeping himself just out of reach. While I debated what to do next, I caught movement from a creek that ran parallel with the open field. A larger buck, which would no doubt meet trophy qualifications, stepped in to join the pursuit.

I would like to go on to say that this foul day buck ended up on my den wall, but unfortunately it didn't go as I had hoped. The bigger buck chased the doe across the creek and into the timber, away from my position. The smaller buck followed, and

I spent the rest of the evening unsuccessfully attempting to intercept them somewhere in the timbers.

Though I was not successful with my stalk, the approaching cold front had proven itself again. The two bucks were out and moving several hours before dark, once again confirming that the change in weather conditions positively affected buck activity.

Stalking is an art that some can do quite well. It takes patience and careful planning to be successful, and I will be the first to admit that I have had my share of problems when trying to do it. Therefore I won't attempt to give instructions on becoming an effective stalker, but I will say that should you prefer to still-hunt, these are the kind of days to do it.

Exceptional stalkers usually prefer windy or rainy conditions, which help drown out unwanted noise and enable the hunter to work their way through the woods without being scented by any deer that may be ahead of them. Many feel they are successful on foul-weather days strictly because of these favorable stalking conditions, but I also believe that it has a lot to do with the increased buck movement that frontal systems seem to trigger. Let's face it: The more bucks that are up and moving, the better opportunity you have to score. A perfect example was mentioned in the preceding paragraphs. While I stalked a smaller buck, a bigger buck moved in. And with a little luck, the cold front could have produced a trophy. It seems likely this event occurred because of the increasing buck activity.

Another plus to hunting on these days is the decrease in hunter activity. Many who might have planned to be in their stands will decide against hunting if it's windy or raining. There are going to be far fewer hunters about, and if buck movement normally increases on these days anyway, there is a far better chance of a buck working his way to you. If you hunt on crowded public lands, this can make a tremendous difference in your hunting success.

One bit of advice is worth mentioning. You should avoid leaving your stand too early on the foul-weather days. On one occasion I learned this the hard way. Again, it was a poor day weather-wise, and the approaching cold front had left me shivering while I was in my morning stand. I left an hour after I had arrived when a light snow began to fall. I returned in the afternoon, better prepared with my clothing, only to find a fresh bed in the snow fifteen yards from my stand. I can't say it was a buck, but one thing is for sure —I will never know.

It is easier to give up on these kind of days, particularly since you may not be seeing the does. You have to be confident that the bucks are moving and that as long as you are in your stand, one of them is going to walk by.

Proper clothing should be considered. I prefer the heavier coveralls, simply because they help to keep the cold wind out, and a ski-type face mask will keep body heat from escaping through your head. I also prefer *polypropylene* or Thinsulate ® long underwear. They are not bulky, and they do an excellent job of keeping you warm while allowing you to draw your bow. If wet conditions exist, by all means cover yourself with some type of rain garment. If you are not comfortable, you are less apt to hang in there, and you won't spend enough time actually hunting. Instead, you spend your time thinking about the cold. Keep spare clothing in your vehicle or camp so you can be ready for these days when they occur.

It is easy for a buck to walk right past you when the wind is blowing, so it is essential that you are continuously watching for deer movement. Most of the bucks I have seen on these days seem to be intent on going somewhere; they never seem to be standing for long periods of time, so you must see them before they pass by. Visibility in bad weather is usually poor, and since a passing buck is not likely to be heard, it is vital you use your eyes and watch all directions.

The weather also can work in your favor once you spot a buck. Since wind causes considerable movement and noise in the woods, brushing your clothing against a tree or quickly

The author tracks a wounded buck, shot with a muzzleloader when the cold front arrived. Photo by Vikki L. Trout

drawing back your bow probably will go unnoticed, where they might not on a still day.

I have noticed on foul days that bucks tend to travel in the really thick cover. The buck mentioned at the beginning of this chapter had evidently come out of a pine thicket and was about to go into an area of dense saplings and honeysuckle. All deer prefer thick cover for protection from bad weather, and during the rut, bucks may assume that this is where they'll find the action they're seeking. Occasionally, however, bucks that are prompted to move will head for open fields to look for does.

I will continue to prefer hunting on the calm days, when it seems as though everything is just right. But when cold fronts move in and a foul day is in the making, I'll plan on being out there just the same. After all, there are just so many days of deer season, and I'm not about to waste any if I can help it.

CHAPTER 10

WHITETAIL ESCAPES

Imagine for just a moment your deer season began in a tree stand overlooking a trail that connected a forest clearing with what seemed like an endless woods. As the hunting pressure intensified, you saw fewer deer. The bucks had completely vanished and obviously headed deeper into the big timber. Although the rut was going strong, the bucks appeared to be nocturnal, leaving their sign on the forest edges only in the middle of the night.

This is common when hunting vast timber areas. Bucks move deep into the safety of huge timber plots until they have reached *no-man's-land*. It is their guarantee of escaping man's intrusion.

But what about farmland bucks that survive year after year when only small woodlots exist? Hunters in these areas are experiencing similar circumstances. When the hunting pressure peaks, the bucks seemingly cease to exist.

HUNTING FARMLAND BUCKS

After too much interference, this buck will look for an escape where hunters seldom venture.

I have hunted whitetails primarily in agricultural habitat for nearly three decades, and many seasons resulted in unfilled tags. My excuses could have filled a magazine page, simply because I would rather take the easy way out than admit that the bucks merely eluded me.

Eventually, however, after having a bad season, I returned the next year during the early archery season and spotted bucks that were more than 1 1/2-years-old. I soon realized that these same bucks were there the previous year, after I had given up. They had survived the hunting pressure by being where I wasn't.

I never fully understood how or why until I began analyzing entire areas after the hunting seasons had ended. Then, upon close examination, I found where the bucks had been hiding and why. Many of these hiding areas were very small and not secluded, but they became escapes for farmland bucks. The escapes were not miles from nowhere. Instead, these hideouts were usually located close to trails I often hunted.

Before we get into the type of areas that become escapes, the hunter should first understand when the bucks are most likely to seek out such hideaways. Farmland bucks are accustomed to human encounters for the most part. Throughout the year, sportsmen are outdoors for various reasons; thus, whitetails are programed to adjust to these meetings to some extent. Farm machinery, barking dogs, kids playing outside, and traffic are everyday events in a farmland buck's life.

Tall weed fields will provide an escape for a pressured buck.

When archery season arrives, human/whitetail confrontations increase. Every time you make a trip to your blind, some scent is left and your presence is known by the deer. This occurs most often in the woodlots that border the fields. This is where hunters are most active, mainly because woodlots are a preferred hunting location. There are generally well-used trails leading from the timber to the fields, not to mention abundant foods along the way.

By the time archery season is about to close, the bucks have become completely aware of areas where humans travel. And if you throw in the first couple of days of the firearm season, many bucks have reached the panic stage. The woodlots that once harbored bucks now become off-limits. The antlered ghosts seem to vanish without any final message, and the hunter is left sitting in a tree stand watching a vacated woods. The fresh sign that was appearing regularly now becomes increasingly stale.

As strange as it might sound, the bucks are still nearby. Their changes are mainly in bedding locations, as well as when they are moving, which is enough to keep a hunter from seeing them.

These so-called hideouts, which I refer to as escapes, are not really difficult to locate if a hunter puts enough effort into finding them. Usually, these are the areas where people rarely venture.

HIGH GRASS FIELDS

It is common to find small patches of broomsage fields in agricultural regions. There are times when these areas are plowed and planted, but most often they are left alone to grow naturally. Also, many states have enacted set-aside programs where farmers are paid not to plant, leaving fields to grow weeds and grasses and providing cover for many species of wildlife.

It doesn't take much of this cover to hide a whitetail buck. Once the weeds have reached a height of two to three feet, it becomes usable habitat for whitetails, particularly since hunters seldom pass through it.

My first encounter of this type of escape came a few years ago while hunting rabbits. Deer season had ended a few days before, and I had no idea the mature weed field was home to a buck. I had hunted deer in a small woodlot bordered by the high grass field on one side and a harvested cornfield on the other. My original assumption was that this particular buck had left the area entirely, but how wrong I was.

I had walked only half of the 200-yard field when I spotted him moving out in front of me. His head was the only thing visible above the tall grass, but still, it was enough to make me feel totally ignorant. The buck had probably been bedding here for a considerable portion of the late season without me knowing it.

By the time I completed walking the field, I had seen a half-dozen whitetails as they flagged their way out of view, and countless beds in the tall grass.

The following year I made it a point to hunt by way of tree stand on the edge of the high grass field where it bordered the back of the woods. The second evening, in early gun season when the pressure was on, I spotted a six-pointer as he attempted to leave the grass field near dusk. He made it only to the timber's edge.

Driving also can be used effectively in these areas. By positioning standers at one end where the timber adjoins the field, the drivers can push the deer to them by starting at the opposite end. If a high vantage point is available, the standers may see deer before they arrive.

HUNTING FARMLAND BUCKS

STANDING CORN

Unfortunately, by the time hunting pressure becomes intense, few cornfields are left standing. Most have been harvested and are providing only a food source. But on rare occasions, because of either wet weather or late harvesting, a field of standing corn may still be around.

I doubt there is anything better to hide a buck than standing corn. They like it at any time, and it offers an excellent escape when the hunting pressure is on. Rows of tall stalks close together can make any buck feel secluded, even when the field is bordered by roads or suburban housing areas. It is a place where few hunters will ever venture, and almost guarantees a buck will be left undisturbed.

Bucks will seek refuge in standing corn fields. Careful stalking can bring home a buck.

Although hunting standing corn can be difficult, many expert stalkers, using bow or gun, love to take on a buck under these conditions. They wait for a windy day that has the dry stalks clapping and making lots of noise. Most hunters claim to walk across the rows with the wind blowing from the direction they are watching, looking up each row in the hope of spotting a bedded buck. Then, using the natural sounds and wind to cover their movement, they stalk the buck until they are within range.

Close examination of the edges will tell you if deer are using the field. Aisles located between the corn and the nearby cover can often be hunted effectively by tree- stand hunters. It is not exactly the kind of place where you will enjoy the scenery, but bucks can be taken here when the escape is being used.

Drivers are not as effective, simply because the hunters cannot see the deer until they are on top of them. Many hunters also find that on some occasions the bucks may not come out of the corn. Instead, they just move from one row to the next to elude the hunters.

DENSE COVER

We all know bucks like thick cover. Many of us don't realize, though, that briar patches, tall full-grown honeysuckle patches, and even blowdowns of timber fall into this type of escape, even when they are neither secluded nor located miles from nowhere.

These types of hideouts are always popular for bucks, but even more so when the hunting pressure is reaching peak intensity all around them. They will often stay there and won't come out, even when hunters pass by at close range.

HUNTING FARMLAND BUCKS

We have all heard tales of how a buck lays there, not flinching a muscle as a hunter passes by. Many of us have seen this happen, and still it remains a phenomenal experience.

Two years ago, my dad had been hunting smack-dab in the middle of thickets and timber bordered by a winter wheat field. Using a muzzleloader, and having no luck, he decided to take his chance in the middle of the open green field. He spotted a fenceline that offered only one location for him to hide in for the evening. It was no more than a 30-yard circle of honeysuckle with a fallen tree in the middle of it. His plans were to settle inside of the stuff and wait for a buck to come into the wheat from the edge of the timber. Dad nearly stepped on a four-pointer as he climbed into the small portion of dense cover. Needless to say, he was caught totally off-guard and never managed to get off a shot as the buck headed for the nearby timber.

Although these small pockets of thick cover are nearly impossible to hunt from tree stands, the hunter may have a chance in the morning hours by arriving well before first light. Simply select the proper location and leave it undisturbed until you are ready.

The stalker, if using the proper techniques, can often do well hunting dense cover escapes. Here, bucks will rely heavily on what they hear and see, often letting the hunter get extremely close. It would be tough for a bowhunter, but the gun hunter may get the easy shot if they are ready when approaching.

SWAMPLANDS

Swamplands often become escapes for the same reasons as fields and dense cover. Few hunters travel this type of terrain, and for good reason. It is extremely noisy when walking it, not

Bucks will not hesitate to hide out in swampy areas.

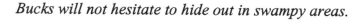

Bucks will not hesitate to hide out in swampy areas.

to mention it is uncomfortably wet and sometimes mosquito-infested.

Wet terrain, however, does not bother bucks the way it does humans. When it comes to survival versus tolerance of wet ground, you can imagine what a buck is going to choose.

These low areas are common in many farmland regions. Even in hilly terrain, there are often a few small, low areas that can easily hide a buck. Sometimes they are overgrown with tall weeds and brush, while other times they are made up of nothing more than a few trees and short grass.

Many areas of the country contain large tracts of swamps, and many expert hunters have learned how to take bucks consistently out of them. Small, low and wet areas also will harbor a buck that, until hunter pressure, traveled other areas. One of these escapes is located along a creek bottom a short distance from my home. Early in the archery season, few deer visit the low-lying areas, but when the surrounding pressure increases, it becomes right with trails and buck rubs.

In south-central Indiana, while hunting the Muscatatuck National Wildlife Refuge, I have seen bucks stand in knee-deep water in an attempt to hide from hunters. These hunters receive a permit in a random drawing, and it takes only a day or two of pressure to send many bucks into the swamps. In most cases, they remain there until the hunting pressure has subsided.

Although I have covered four basic escape areas that are commonly found in agricultural regions, your area may offer something entirely different. One possibility is a strip-mined area. When coal was extracted from certain regions several years ago, the ground was left uprooted. Tall mounds, some reaching 30 feet or higher, became overgrown with trees and brush. Since these areas are seldom traveled by man, deer naturally use them for escapes. Most hunters stick to hunting the edges of these areas, simply because the terrain is too rough to hunt. However, this is precisely why bucks favor these escapes.

Regardless of where you are in farmland country, there are sure to be escapes that will be appealing to bucks. Even during the rut, when conditions exist to make a buck nocturnal, the hunter's chances are considerably better when hunting near the escapes.

Perhaps all of the tactics previously mentioned could be better understood if we think like a farmland buck. They simply do what it takes to avoid those areas that threaten their everyday survival. Instead, they head for areas that are the most unappealing to us.

(Portions of this chapter was reprinted with permission from Petersen Publishing Company.)

CHAPTER 11

HUNTING THE LATE SEASON

Hunting the late season, whether it be with gun or bow, differs from the early season tremendously. There are drastic changes in the buck's habits, and the hunter must apply different techniques to be successful.

Many states now have extended or split seasons to accommodate both the muzzleloading and/or archery enthusiast. Bag limits during this period are often no different from the earlier seasons, and the hunter sometimes has the once-crowded public areas to themselves. Many do not brave the cold weather, and most assume the chances of success grow slimmer with each passing day.

Although there were years that I would have been better off to hang it up when the first round ended, I always continued if I carried an unused tag. I hunt seriously with bow and gun (including a muzzleloader), and any opportunity to head for the woods is my objective. Although some of my late-season hunts have ended in failures, I have now adjusted to the different

141

techniques that are necessary, and have enjoyed enough success during the cold months to make it worth my while.

There is no doubt, you must have a complete understanding of the buck's habits. This is essential for success, simply because they are changing a little each day. These changes include the food sources, the late rut and the gathering of whitetails that we refer to as *yarding*.

After Jack Frost arrives, the whitetail's range begins to change. I have seen bedding areas used consistently in the early fall become deserted by late November or early December. The food sources are also affected. Many agricultural offerings have now dwindled, and the whitetail turns to any type of food offering found within its range.

The hunter can take advantage of this situation if he or she knows where the whitetail will feed. They will often become programed to feed at nearly the same time each day, which is why I prefer to hunt the food sources late in the season. If I do my homework and hunt consistently, I can expect to see 2 to 3 times as many deer as I would have in the early season.

One drawback is in the number of bucks that still roam the area. As the old saying goes, ''There ain't quite as many as there was awhile ago.''

The regular firearm season is responsible for the harvest of the most bucks in any state. These figures will often represent 75 percent or more of the total whitetail harvest. This means you will not have the selection of antlered bucks that you had during the earlier season. It also means you have to scout more and hunt harder to be successful. The available food sources, however, will make the job easier.

In an earlier chapter I covered several food sources. They included honeysuckle, winter wheat and red oak acorns. Each of these offers food in the late season, and any can provide you with hunting opportunities. Other late season foods also can

Many states offer a muzzleloading season after the regular firearm season has ended. Those who continue to hunt vigorously may enjoy the remainder of the season without experiencing hunting pressure.

143

When the yarding begins, it is not uncommon to see several deer in one agricultural field. These deer are feeding on winter wheat, a favored late-season food source.

work in your favor. Deer feed on whatever is available. There are preferred foods, but when they no longer exist the whitetail will turn to whatever it can find.

Several years ago I was traveling a backroad just after the season had closed. At least four inches of snow was on the ground, and had been for many days. I came across a harvested cornfield that I had not seen a deer in for a couple of months. Surprisingly, I counted 27 deer that allowed me to pull over and observe them for the next 30 minutes. The deer were feeding heavily on the corn stubbles that protruded above the snow.

I am sure they were doing so only because it was available. It certainly had not been a reliable food source in the previous weeks. I had driven past the field on a regular basis for quite some time, and had not seen deer in this field until the snow had been on the ground.

The best way to locate a late season food source is to cover as much ground as you can. If you plan on hunting a weekend, you may need a preceding weekend just to find a suitable location. However, if you have been a consistent late season hunter in previous years, it may be possible to return to the same areas and achieve results.

I know of a few areas where very little time is needed for scouting. The same food is available each year in the winter months, and seldom do I have to make a major move.

One fenceline I have hunted borders a pine thicket on one side, and contains a stretch of several pin oaks on the other. The small bitter acorns usually start falling sometime in October and often continue through December. Several trails cross the fenceline to provide hunting opportunities during the entire season. A good friend of mine has taken several bucks in this area. His success is attributed to the habitat and excellent trails that meander back and forth across the fenceline. It is a natural area for the deer to use. The deer never actually hit the available acorns until December. But when they do, the area quickly becomes hot, and you can usually count on seeing several deer simply because of the available food. As for the bucks, they often show up with the other deer.

I am gifted to live in an area where honeysuckle is abundant—perhaps too gifted. There is so much available that the deer do not become reliable at any particular thicket. On occasion, though, the deer do become consistent with certain pockets of the dark green vegetation. Many times I have located these areas and found very few of the honeysuckle leaves remaining on the vines.

Winter wheat also provides excellent food for the white-tail late in the season. But many deer in the Midwest do not prefer to eat wheat until it is a have-to situation. Most of the time something else will be available, but it does pay to keep a close eye on this food source. It can become a hotspot overnight.

Snow will increase your chances tremendously when hunting a food source. And if it is on the ground for several days, it is possible to see an increase in buck movement on a daily basis.

The hunter also should spend more hours actually hunting when snow covers the ground. Although weather conditions might affect how long you can stick it out, it will pay to be prepared with the proper clothing and footwear. Some

Whitetails find protection from harsh winter weather in thick cover, as well as browse when other foods are not available.

Most of the scraping has subsided by the time the late-season hunting arrives. This buck, however, may have been provoked by a late-estrous doe.

whitetail bucks are spotted during the late season at various hours of the day. If you can spend an extra hour in your stand during the morning and afternoon, you probably will see a difference in the frequency of deer movement.

Snow also will turn the deer to higher browse. Many agricultural food sources no longer attract deer because the food has been covered, logically speaking. However, whitetails will paw through the snow to search for acorns or other browse whenever possible. This usually occurs when the snow reaches a depth of several inches. I have seen the woods near several red oak thickets pawed so much that they resembled turkey scratchings.

Keep in mind that the habits of the bucks do not differ all that much from the does and fawns, except that they can and will often breed if the opportunity arrives during the mid-winter months. Does that did not breed earlier, and doe fawns that come into estrous late will attract bucks.

The scraping has usually subsided by this time, although this can vary with geographical locations and the number of bucks in an area. Whenever I notice the competition is strong, I see scrapes show up in the post-rut period. Rubbing also will decrease, but it does not stop.

A few years ago on the last day of Indiana's archery season, several deer approached my stand. About 60 yards before they reached me, two bucks began to quarrel while the does and fawns watched the action. Out of nowhere came an even bigger buck and joined them. The fighting stopped when one of the bucks began chasing a mature doe. I did not get a chance to draw my bow, but I did enjoy the action.

Although this incident was rare for this time of year in this area, it did prove the biological fact that a buck will think about breeding at any time. And this event, along with similar reactions I have experienced, has convinced me that a doe in estrous late in the season will attract several bucks.

I have also enjoyed some success calling to bucks during the late season but it has not been a reliable method. On several occasions I have called, using either a grunt or bleat, and had a passing buck pay me little or no attention.

I prefer to hunt in the thick stuff during the entire season, but I believe it is most important during the late archery season. The bucks just seem to be attracted to dense cover in the winter months for several reasons.

A buck may ease up his nocturnal instincts during the mid-winter months.

One major factor is the protection from the harsh winter weather. Although I seldom see much snow in the Midwest, cold winds are still enough to keep the deer in the protective cover of brush, pines or whatever else it can find.

Another reason many bucks will remain in the thick cover is due to the earlier hunting pressure. They used these areas for security when it became necessary, and it offered them a retreat where there were no interruptions.

The difference, however, lies in their nocturnal habits. The bucks will begin leaving the bedding areas earlier in the afternoon, and get back to them later in the mornings. Their overall movements increase because of little or no hunting pressure, and the need to feed more often.

Southern Indiana bowhunter, John Benetti, has been very successful during the late season. According to Benetti, the late season is an excellent time to score on bucks if enough scouting goes into locating them. He often forfeits hunting time to find them.

I have to agree. The hunter must be willing to put an effort into finding the bucks. Driving roads is a good start. You will be surprised how many more bucks can be seen in fields after the hunting pressure subsides. It also will help to talk to school bus drivers and mail carriers. They spend about every day traveling the backroads and are sure to see bucks occasionally if they are in the area.

The key is to know where the bucks are moving. Unlike the rut, they will not be covering as much ground as they normally do. This means they have more home range and can be patterned much easier. Bucks that may have traveled two or three miles during the rut may now limit their movements to a mile or less.

The term *yarding* stems from deer gathering in deer yards. The reason deer yard up is to conserve energy. In many northern states, deer migrations during the winter have traditionally affected whitetails to move several miles. Their yards can take place on mountain sides, meadows, or even a small forest opening.

Many hunters in farmland country often spot several deer together in the winter months, and refer to them as *yarded* up. This is not really the case, but it does happen in such a way that resembles the yarding that takes place in the north. The deer do not move a considerable distance, but it is common to see several together.

Deer trails always look better in the winter months. This is due to the sparse amount of vegetation and the number of deer using a particular trail. Imagine what a group of 6 to 8 deer will do to a trail if they walk it in single file.

Unfortunately we will often choose these trails to hunt, even though the deer may not travel them regularly. This reason prompts me to hunt the food sources during the late season. It just seems more logical to place my stand at an active location than to take a chance on a trail that simply looks good. I still

Several deer traveling together will make any trail look good.

choose trails to hunt, but I restrict my selections to those close to the food.

Many of us have voiced a strong opinion in the last few years about baiting deer. It is legal in a few states, and it can make a difference in success or failure.

First off, I should add that it is not legal in Indiana where I reside. It is, however, legal in Kentucky which is only a 30-minute drive from my home. I don't bait deer in either state, but if it were legal in Indiana I probably would participate during the late season.

I have enjoyed bear hunting over baits for more years than I can remember. For several years I have hunted both the spring and fall seasons in Canada, and I have also traveled to the Rocky Mountains to bait blackies. Although I have enjoyed several successful hunts, none have come easy. Each hunt required a great deal of hard work. Many techniques were tried, and several failed. It is not just a matter of throwing out a pile of garbage, nor is it that easy to bait whitetails successfully.

Corn is probably the most popular choice for baiting deer. Whitetails will consistently feed on it whenever certain conditions exist. The main factor is weather, which makes the winter months prime time for baiting.

When starting a bait, it is important to keep a food supply available. I know of many baiters who begin with 50 pounds or more, and keep it replenished before the supply expires. Although it is usually placed on the ground, some hunters prefer the barrel feeders that are time-released. They will dispense the feed as needed, usually at sunrise and sunset.

The hunter can select an area according to how they may want to hunt. You can choose a location where a hill will not cause you to be scented by approaching deer. You can even select an area that will allow you to place your stand on either side of the bait. This will give you an alternative when the wind direction changes. You will, however, need to place your bait where it can be found. Of course this means you must still locate an area the deer are using frequently.

Deer also can be led to your bait. I have experienced this while baiting wild turkeys for photography during the winter months. I usually place the baits in an area where light can enter. Sometimes this requires me to run a trail of corn to my bait. I have done this for distances of 200 to 300 yards, and have had both turkeys and deer follow it directly to the main bait station.

Some hunters claim that baiting deer does not differ from hunting over an acorn tree or an agricultural field that attracts deer. However, I have to disagree with this. A bait will no doubt draw deer more consistently when other food is not available, and it will put them in your lap. I strongly favor baiting, and would suspect that more states may legalize it in the future, particularly when it comes to the late archery season. It is certainly not going to mean that a major portion of the deer herd would be reduced, especially if it is legal only during the late seasons.

As for hunting bucks, bait can be an effective method. It is a food source, and in my opinion there is not a better place to find a buck during the late season.

A doe that was not bred is sure to attract a buck during the late season.

CHAPTER 12

HUNTING TROPHY BUCKS

I have never met a deer hunter who didn't want to take a record-book whitetail. Each hunter thinks about it, and many have been fortunate enough to experience the thrill. Whether we are just a deer hunter, ready to take whatever legal deer that comes along, or a hunter after any buck, we always hold a special thought in the back of our mind that includes a monster buck appearing out of nowhere.

I would speculate that most record book whitetails are taken by *lucky* hunters. Perhaps that was not said in good taste. Maybe I should have said that most are taken by hunters who would have been happy to have taken any legal buck. Actually, we luck into very few whitetails, regardless of their size. When an avid deer hunter is successful, he/she usually earns it. But I do believe that many individuals who have taken a trophy buck did so because they were in the right area on the right day.

Simply said, they were not hunting that specific big buck. And many times these same hunters did not know that a buck of that size was in the area.

There are a special few, though, who have taken several big boys repeatedly. These individuals know what they are doing, and have earned a spot in the *Whitetail Hall Of Fame,* if such a thing ever comes to be.

Although I have never been a consistent, successful trophy hunter, I have learned that there are two necessary ingredients required to take big bucks regularly; hard work and the right area.

I have done several interviews with successful trophy hunters. Surprisingly, many of them use different techniques. Whether they hunt with bow or gun, each gives different opinions that contribute to their success. Not surprising, however, is the areas they hunt, and the amount of effort that must go into pursuing trophy bucks. These individuals work very hard and put every possible spare minute into hunting. And each does not waste time hunting where big bucks do not exist.

Although money may have something to do with trophy hunting, mainly because it can put you on the best ranch in Texas, it does not mean that all consistent trophy hunters are loaded with greenbacks. On the contrary, most do it on private lands near their homes with no extra fee included for a record-book deer. Travel and license fees are the main costs. Many that hunt their home state travel to a neighboring state for an extra opportunity.

We all know that very few states, as far as public land is concerned, offers potential for trophy hunting. The bulk of the harvests are 1 1/2-year-old bucks, and very few reach a mature stage.

Trophy hunting requires hard work and persistence. But first you must also know that a mature buck exists in the area you plan to hunt.

I am not knocking public land hunting. As a matter of fact, some of my time is spent on public land each season, or shared on a hunting lease where few big bucks exist. But I am aware that private land, particularly the large tracts, open a door to the trophy hunter. Many big bucks take refuge in these areas when the pressure becomes intense. You often get the opportunity to hunt alone while the bucks are functioning normal. By that I mean they are less nocturnal. This increases buck

157

movement, and offers a better opportunity for the hunter to use patience and wait for a big buck.

At the time of this writing I am about to enter a whitetail into the Pope & Young records. I took the buck during a 1-week hunt in Alberta, only a half-hour drive from the big city of Edmonton. The buck scored 141 points, and was the third Pope & Young buck I had seen during the six days I spent in the province. Although I have hunted Indiana consistently for more than 30 years, I had never taken a deer equal to that buck. The area in Alberta, however, does not allow rifle hunting. It is a selected area called the *bow- zone*, and is large enough to allow bucks to mature, as long as the whitetails do not over-populate. I should add, though, that guides are required.

A large portion of the bow-zone in Alberta is farmland, and many big bucks, both Pope & Young and Boone & Crockett, have come from the area. Just prior to starting this chapter, there were reports of a possible new world record from Alberta, pending the official scoring and paper work.

There is no way of knowing how many record book bucks come from farmland areas, but I would speculate that several do.

No doubt, the big timber areas hide a few of the whoppers, but the farmland offers everything a buck needs to grow a big rack, providing it lives long enough.

M. J. Johnson still holds the number one spot in the Pope & Young records with the Illinois buck that scored 204 4/8. I also should say, the **Bowhunting Big Game Records, Second Edition**, published by the Pope & Young Club in 1981, showed the number 2 and 3 spots belonged to Iowa. Iowa and Illinois are agricultural states. Other states in the top 20 listings include Nebraska, Kansas, Minnesota, Ohio and South Dakota. I believe this says a great deal about the trophy potential of farmland bucks.

In the most recent supplement published by the Pope & Young Club, **Seventeenth Recording Period 1989-1990**, Michigan received the number 1 spot in the *Typical Whitetails* with a buck entered by Craig Calderone. The buck scored 193 2/8, and came from Jackson County in the southern farmland portion.

The leading state in the top 20 from the two-year entry period is Iowa with six. Iowa received the number 2, 6, 7, 9, 13 and 19 spots. Kansas came through with three entries, while Ohio and Illinois managed to grab two rankings each. Other states with entries include Delaware, Wisconsin, Missouri and Montana.

Listed in the same recording period are individual states and the total number of entries. Surprisingly, Wisconsin had 1,003 entries. However, more than half scored between 125 - 134 points. Illinois added 770 entries, Minnesota 599, Iowa 500, Kansas 498, and Ohio 440.

Illinois had 161 entries that scored between 145 - 154, and 93 that scored between 155 - 164. Iowa furnished 72, and Kansas 64 bucks in the 155 -164 class.

As for the really big bucks, those that scored between 175 - 184 P & Y points, Kansas took all honors with 13 entries. Minnesota followed with 8, and Iowa with 7 entries.

In the *Non-typical Whitetails*, Minnesota recorded 55, Kansas 49, Iowa and Illinois 42, and Wisconsin 40.

Several factors play a role in the growth of antlers. Nutrition is a major factor, and it may be necessary for a buck to reach trophy scoring potential. Many bucks that receive the proper nutrition can surpass the Pope & Young minimum score when they are 3 1/2-years-old. However, if they do not receive the necessary nutrition, it may set the antler growth back a year or more. And in areas where the range is exceptionally poor, they may never reach trophy potential. The proper soil nutrition must consist of both phosphorus and calcium. Another neces-

HUNTING FARMLAND BUCKS

Genetics does not necessarily play a role in spikes. This 1 1/2-year-old buck could grow large antlers in future years with the proper nutrition.

sary ingredient is moisture. The soil must receive enough rainfall to insure growth of forage.

One area in Indiana is a prime example. The Muscatatuck National Wildlife Refuge has produced several monster bucks. The area is swampy, and the right ingredients are found in the soil.

Genetics also may be a factor. I can't say for sure, mainly because biologists still argue about the genetic influence of related bucks. We used to hear that the spikes should be culled. We were told they were inferior, and that leaving them would most certainly lead to more spikes. But things have changed. Captive 1 1/2-year-old spikes turned into trophy bucks when they were 3 1/2-years-old, after being fed a nutritional diet. Perhaps the most interesting evidence lies in the whitetail race. Northern and Dakota whitetails commonly produce high numbers of trophy bucks.

The population density also may contribute to the number of trophy bucks. Too many deer will lead to fewer trophy bucks, simply because of the unavailable nutritional foods. A low whitetail population will eat less. Thus, there will be far

Indiana bowhunter John Benetti with a 1990 buck that scored 167 3/8. Photo by John Benetti.

more nutritional food available that is needed to produce large antlers. Many agricultural areas meet the nutritional necessities, but as deer herds continue to expand, these same areas may begin producing fewer trophy bucks. Hopefully, depredation permits will help this situation as time goes on.

Becoming a trophy hunter often occurs after a hunter takes their first. Southern Indiana bowhunter John Benetti began deer hunting about 30 years ago. He took his first trophy whitetail in 1987, and followed with three more from 1988 to 1991.

Benetti claims that it was his ability to "hold out for the big ones" that have made a difference. He also says that the hunter must know where a big buck is located. He relies on locating sheds during the winter months.

Once he has found a big buck, Benetti concentrates on several locations to ambush the buck. He never relies on one location. When the wind changes, so does he.

Benetti also claims that the late season is an excellent time to take a trophy buck, particularly when snow is on the ground. According to Benetti, the big bucks are not as nocturnal, and their feeding habits increase. He warns, though, that the hunter must be very careful and not let a buck know of your presence when walking in and out of the agricultural areas.

Royce Frazier of Haviland, Kansas began deer hunting in 1977, and took his first trophy buck in 1985. The non-typical buck scored an amazing 181 Pope & Young points.

Frazier followed with several more Pope & Young bucks, including two in 1987. The best, a non-typical scoring 232 7/8, earned him the number two spot for non-typicals of 1987 at the Pope & Young Club banquet held in Boise, Idaho. The huge buck had 20 points, and an inside spread of 20 6/8 inches.

Kansas bowhunter Royce Frazier took five trophy bucks in six years.   Photo by Royce Frazier.

Frazier also claims that locating a big buck plays a major role in trophy hunting success.

"Early in the season I locate scrapes and set up in whatever kind of tree I can find that gives me a broad view of the area. Our season lasts for about three months, and in the beginning weeks the only thing I care about is seeing the bucks that are there. Once I know where a big one is located, I can start hunting him," said Frazier.

Nationally known and highly successful bowhunter Myles Keller has hunted the farmlands of many states. He also claims that locating a big buck is the first step, and says a good pair of binoculars or a spotting scope is most useful.

"I think it is one of the easiest ways to hunt, and I use it as a safety valve," said Keller. "If you have a limited food source, the deer can be spotted easily."

Keller stressed the importance, though, of not acting too quickly.

"Many hunters will get anxious to hunt and run into an area and throw up a tree stand right away," explained Keller.

Keller has hunted Iowa for several years, and relies on binoculars to do a large part of his scouting. He even sacrifices hunting time so that he can locate other bucks when the rut is close. This allows him to spot bucks entering fields, and the doe chasing that often occurs in the open areas, providing the activity is not completely nocturnal.

Keller also feels that to hunt successfully, you must hunt when the wind is in your favor.

"Even experienced hunters will sometimes hunt against the wind," said Keller, claiming that many good set-ups have been ruined because of this.

Keller says that he, too, has cut corners and took chances when the wind was not in his favor, but claims that most of the time it will catch up to you.

Keller remains cautious of his approach when hunting big bucks, and admits he wishes he could drop out of the sky and into the stand. But when he concentrates on a particular buck, he settles for one stand in that area only. He doesn't try to use several stands in the same area of cover he expects the buck to be. He then forces himself to hunt it only when the wind is right.

Keller has hunted the edges and the thick stuff, and has had success in both. He judges this by the wariness of the bucks he hunts. He has seen some difference in the big bucks of Iowa compared to those in Minnesota, but claims you still have to hunt using the right approach, and when the wind favors the hunter.

Being able to field-judge a buck accurately in the field is crucial. Many hunters can make these decisions quickly, simply because they have a considerable amount of experience. But few of us see bucks in the trophy class regularly. We are geared to see 1 1/2-year-old bucks.

In many cases, only a few seconds are offered to field-judge a buck. Seldom does this short time span give us a

Low, wide racks seldom score as high as tall, narrow racks.

165

complete view of the buck's head-gear. We may see only one side of the rack, and when coupled with a moving deer in dense cover, it can be almost impossible to estimate a score.

You can gain experience by visiting scoring sessions and taxidermy studios. You will get the chance to estimate a buck's score, and test your accuracy.

Most of us already know the Pope & Young typical whitetail minimum score is 125. The Boone & Crockett minimum is 170 respectively. Like many hunters, I have found it more difficult to judge Boone & Crockett bucks. Those that score in the 130s and 140s are much more common, and far easier to estimate.

Most hunters are more impressed when they see a wide rack, but a good inside spread does not always mean a buck will score high. My best buck was just under 16 inches. It scored 141 in the typical class. I have taken others, though, that had inside spreads of 18 and 19 inches that did not score as high.

This was due to either shorter points, less beam length and mass. Normally, a high-narrow rack will score more than low-wide antlers, but this rule only stands when the necessary factors exist. The best way to judge width is to compare the spread with the ears. When a mature buck expands their ears in an alert position, they should have a spread of about 15 inches. If the antlers extend one inch beyond each ear tip, the buck should have an inside antler spread of about 17 inches. Large-bodied deer, though may have an ear-spread of 16 or 17 inches.

Sometimes we see a buck only from the broadside view. But the broadside view allows us to judge the number of points, the main beam length, and the amount of mass in many situations.

To judge the length of the main beam, compare it to the head of the buck and to the tip of its nose. Most mature bucks will have a total head length of about 25 inches. If you view a main beam that appears to stop two inches in front of the nose, you can assume the main beam length is about 23 inches.

Any point one inch or larger will qualify as a keeper. Both the number of points and their lengths will affect the final score. When a buck is walking, I concentrate on both the number and length of the points. On a running deer, though, it can be almost impossible to estimate the number. Therefore, when a buck is moving through quickly, or in thick cover that allows very little visibility, I concentrate on the length of the points.

If you count the points standing upright on a broadside deer, you can usually make an accurate assumption. An 8-pointer will have two points, a 10-pointer three points, and a 12-pointer will have four points visible. The end of the main beam should not be included, even though it will count as a point when the rack is scored. Another point can be added for the brow tine.

The length of the point will usually add more to the final score than the number of points. For example, a 10-pointer with short points could easily be outscored by an 8-pointer with long points.

Impressive height, especially points that measure 10 inches or longer, are much more noticeable on bucks when they are white. However, dark colored racks are not uncommon, and an allowance should be considered, especially when a deer is moving or standing in cover.

Again, it is the deer's head that offers the best method to judge the length of the points. A mature buck's ears will usually be 6 to 7 inches long when they are in the alert position. The hunter can use two techniques to compare the points with the length of the ears. They can select the longest point and compare it to the ear. If it appears to be the same length as the ear, one could assume it is a 6 to 7-inch point.

The other method is to judge how much of the point rises above the ear. Usually a point begins off the main beam about

167

This 8-pointer is a little short of the Pope & Young minimum score. Many deer hunters would find it hard to pass this buck. However, a dedicated trophy hunter would wait for bigger antlers.

halfway up the ear. If it looks like three inches stick above the ear, it might be safe to assume that the point is about six inches total. The largest tine is generally the first past the brow tine. If you spot a buck that has good length on this point, and another point or two that is close to this length, you can bet the buck will score high.

Judging mass can be a bit more difficult. I have found the best technique is to spend time looking at mounted heads. Heavy mass does have a distinct look, even in the field when compared to bucks with spindly antlers.

There is nothing embarrassing about missing an estimated score by a long-shot. Very few individuals can judge a trophy buck within a couple of inches consistently. I often find myself way out of the ball park on bucks that surpass the 150-class. I do consider it to be an exciting challenge, though, whether I am in the field or observing a measurement session.

Trophy hunting is not for those who want to harvest deer consistently. It takes dedication, hard work, the ability to look past the small bucks, and an open mind when you come home empty-handed.

The antlers of this buck extend the width of the ears. His spread is estimated at 15 inches.

CHAPTER 13

PHOTOGRAPHING FARMLAND BUCKS

Just about every deer hunter enjoys shooting photos when it involves a white-tailed buck. Whether you photograph a deer in a soybean field down the road from where you live, or get a few shots for the scrapbook of the buck you harvested, there is sure to be a memory captured.

Good quality photos, however, require some knowledge of cameras, lenses, film, patience and an understanding of the deer. Cost is optional. You can invest a few weekly paychecks if you desire, or you can stick with inexpensive equipment and still get respectable photographs.

When I started shooting photographs in the early 1980s, I became obsessed with equipment improvements and spending time in the field. I quickly learned, persistence was the key to getting good photographs that had marketable potential.

Regardless of whether you hope to sell your photos, I will provide enough information and suggestions in this chapter to help you begin, or improve your present photography abilities.

The deer hunter often mixes the hunting and photography. On several occasions I have taken my camera, lenses and bow or gun into my tree stand. However, I have found they seldom work together. Deer have approached my ambush location and offered a photographing opportunity, and a chance for me to harvest the animal. Normally, I can't make up my mind whether I should grab the weapon or camera. By the time I've made the decision, the animal has already passed or spotted my movement.

I do most of my buck photography along fields prior to the hunting season, or in parks where hunting is prohibited. Bucks that are hunted offer fewer opportunities, and finding enough time to spend waiting for them often becomes impossible.

There is one misconception about whitetail photography. To obtain a good quality photograph, perhaps one that is marketable, it usually takes more than a single exposure. When I capture a deer on film, I continue to shoot as long as the animal is within camera range. I never assume that I have taken a superb photo after shooting only a few frames.

Most magazine photos, particularly the mature bucks, are taken in areas where deer have little fear of man. These photos will appear with normal habitat. But this does not necessarily mean that good photos of these deer are easy to come by. On the contrary, you also must have some knowledge about exposures and lighting. Second, a good understanding of the animal will help you predict what might happen next. Most of the country's leading wildlife photographers are knowledgeable of their subjects.

State and national parks that do not allow hunting will help your photography abilities. You can often shoot a great

The author captured this photograph along the fringe as the small buck paused to look over a nearby soybean field.

deal of film in a few hours time. This will help you to see what mistakes you have made when viewing your photos at a later date.

The late-summer months offer possibilities in many farmland areas that receive hunting pressure. Although the bucks will still carry the velvet, you may obtain excellent photographs by setting up in the right areas and waiting for the bucks to appear. At this time of the year, the deer often visit the fields with some regularity in daylight hours. However, after the hunting begins, the deer are forced into their natural, nocturnal habits.   And as you know, the daylight visitations to the agricultural fields quickly comes to a halt.

Any field that has become a regular stopover for the deer will offer an opportunity. I do very well in soybean fields in late July and early August. The lush, green leaves of the plants are a favorite in mid-summer, and action can usually be expected. In many areas of the south, the soybeans are visited regularly by the whitetail as late as September and October.

Many landowners that do not give permission to hunt will allow you to do photography. I often ask permission to set up a photo blind in the agricultural areas where hunting is not allowed. Occasionally, a friendly relationship begins that may eventually lead to a hunting opportunity.

A dome tent will make an excellent photo blind.

A photo blind will help you get the desired shots without distracting your subject.

When I work the fields with my camera where I will soon be hunting, it usually helps my early season scouting. If I spend a few evenings along a field, it doesn't take long for me to see how many bucks are in the area. I also can determine if there are any wall-hangers, or other respectable bucks that I may decide to pursue.

Most antlered bucks stick together in the summer months, and it is not uncommon to see several together. Both the mature and young bucks may group separately. But the photographer must set up close to where the bucks enter a field to obtain the best photos. Since deer browse naturally, they will usually move away from your position and out of range of your lens quickly.

Baits may produce excellent results, providing they are legal where you do your photography. I have baited with both corn and apples but the amount of available natural food will play a role in how often the deer visit your bait. I have my best results over baits in the winter months. This is usually due to a lack of available, natural foods.

I prefer to place the bait no more than 50 yards from where I will be positioned, and occasionally closer. I also spread the bait over an area to force the deer to separate. This helps to frame one deer properly, and to keep part of another out of the photograph. If there is one buck that I attempt to photograph, it helps to keep the does or a smaller buck in a separate location. But I do shoot photos of the does and fawns. However, no matter how many deer visit the bait, you must remain undetected.

I have used natural blinds made from limbs and other debris, but the tent blind has provided me with the best photography. In the natural blinds, including those where camo netting is used, I am often spotted or smelled. When hunting with a weapon, the natural blind is a better choice since I only have to make one shot count. But when using the camera it may take several photos to obtain something good, and a long period of time to get them. Normally the whitetail must get used to the unnatural blind. More about that in a moment.

Dome tents will make an excellent blind, and offer some convenience. If you are caught in the rain, you can simply sit back and wait for it to pass. Most can be erected easily and quietly in a few minutes.

You can buy the inexpensive, smaller 4 to 5-foot dome tents for under $40. One company makes a camo dome tent that sells for about $60. Keep in mind, these small tents are not the best, but will serve the purpose very well. And if you don't mind painting, you can do a spray-job on the less expensive tents to remove the natural glare that accompanies them.

Unfortunately, you must cut a hole in the dome tent to allow an opening for your lens. That may not sound practical, but you can forget about using the door or windows for your opening. They are normally to large. I cut a hole in the side of the tent slightly larger than the barrel of the lens. When I settle into the blind, I use a small seat. The seat will allow me to spend several hours comfortably waiting for the action, and help me remain still.

A blind should be placed in the area long before you hope to spend time there. Deer will normally get used to the

It pays to carry your camera along whenever you are in the field. This unusual, white buck allowed the author to get a rare photograph.

oddity that has invaded their territory, but it may require several days. Strangely, I have had wild turkeys come in very close the same day I set up the blind. Deer, however, usually remain cautious until they have passed by several times.

Equipment should be considered as the most important part of anyone's photography. This does not necessarily mean that one should buy the most expensive cameras and lenses available. More important is that you should have the proper equipment for the photography you want to do, and understand how to use it effectively.

Most serious photographers prefer a 35 MM camera. The disk or instamatic are not preferred for many reasons. However, one major factor is negative size. The 35 MM negative is considerably larger and allows you to produce better photos when enlarged.

There are a couple of different types of 35 MM cameras, as well as several brands available. One is completely automatic. Thus, the camera does all the work. It is simply a point and shoot situation. The camera picks the proper exposure and focuses. Many brands make cameras of this type that are available at reasonable prices. If one is wanting to use a camera for the purpose of just taking shots of their trophies, they are hard to beat. You can use several different speeds of film, adjusted for the amount of light available, and produce excellent photographs.

If you are wanting to consider wildlife photography along with the rest, I would recommend a 35 MM camera that allows you to interchange lenses. The point/shoot cameras are not suitable for wildlife, since it is necessary to have your subject appear closer. But if you have a camera capable of using several lenses, you will be increasing opportunities. It is just a matter of deciding what will best suit your needs. Before making your decision, it is best to borrow a camera or discuss it with those who are familiar with both types.

If your choice is to buy the more sophisticated 35 MM camera that allows you to interchange lenses, be prepared for a wide range of prices. Most all brands will allow you to take good photographs if you learn to use the equipment correctly. Most often, it is the person behind the equipment that determines the quality of the photograph.

These cameras normally come with a standard 50 MM lens. It will be fine for shots of you and your trophy and most hunting scenes. Wide angle lenses from 20 MM to 35 MM will often help the photographer to create a more sparkling picture, but they are not necessary.

When choosing a lens for photographing deer, you will almost certainly become confused. You must first understand the features which separate them.

You have the option of purchasing a zoom lens or a fixed telephoto. One example of a popular zoom is a lens which ranges from 80-200 MM. This allows the photographer to zoom in if the subject is far, or zoom out if it is too close.

The telephoto lens is a single-focal fixed lens. You cannot move your subject further or closer. Instead, it is the photographer that has to move.

I have been asked on many occasions, "How far were you from that deer?"

A full-body photo of a deer that has been framed properly would include some surrounding terrain. If the deer took up 1/3 to 1/2 of the frame it would look acceptable. With a 200 MM lens, the deer would need to be about 20 to 25 yards from the photographer. A 400 MM would capture a similar framed shot at 40 to 50 yards. A tightly framed head-shot of a buck, for example, would need to be within 15 to 20 yards if you used a 400 MM lens. Many tend to think that published photographs are shot from several hundred yards. However, no lens will allow you to do this and receive a quality photograph.

Although I own several lenses, my favorite is the 400 MM telephoto. I use it most often when I travel, and when working in blinds near agricultural fields. I can place the blind as far as desired from the bait or trail to allow the proper framing. A 300 MM telephoto is also a popular choice, and not as expensive as the larger, 400 MM lens.

A lens can be either slow or fast. A fast lens, however, does not mean it is necessarily better. A fast lens allows you to shoot in lower light conditions, but they are also heavier, more expensive, and normally require a tripod to prevent movement that can blur your photograph.

A lens will have an aperture setting on the barrel that determines how fast it will be. These are called f stops. A lens that has a low f stop number, around f 2.8 to f 4.5, will be faster than one at f 8. The lower the number the larger the opening, and the faster you can shoot. Many zoom lens which extend to 200 MM with an f stop down to 3.8 or 4.5 can be purchased for under $150. A 400 MM lens with an f stop down to 2.8 may sell for a few thousand dollars.

The type of film you shoot is also an important factor. You can shoot slides or print film in a variety of speeds. These speeds are marked on the box. The lower the number, the slower the film, which means more light is needed. But keep in mind, if you are shooting fast speed film in low light, the photograph will usually have a grainy appearance.

I shoot mostly slide film with an ASA/ISO rating of 64. Slow slide film such as this will produce good quality photographs. However, I use this because it is what most publications prefer. But I am restricted to shooting when light is available. Even on a sunny day, I will normally have to stop an hour before dark. If I'm interested in photographs of wildlife and trophies for my personal scrapbook, I choose to shoot print film in faster speeds. Slides can be converted to prints but it is costly.

Print film can range from ASA/ISO 100 to 1000. When I do shoot prints, I generally choose the ASA/ISO 100 or 200. If you expect to take photos where little light is present, the faster ASA/ISO 400 is a good choice. Although it will be grainy, you are more certain of getting a sharp photograph. It works well in most hunting situations, simply because a dark, overcast day will not interfere.

Excellent photographs are often created by the photographer. The equipment may contribute toward the possibilities, but the individual will determine the overall outcome.

Once the hunting begins, a trophy buck isn't likely to venture into open fields and offer photographing opportunities.

HUNTING FARMLAND BUCKS

A hunting trip can be better remembered if one uses their imagination. Not always is it best just to shoot photos of the hunter and deer. Consider the country you are in and shoot photos of a fellow hunter somewhere off to one side, rather than centering the subject. Shoot photos of your buddies looking at buck rubs, scrapes, trails or hanging their tree stands. Perhaps a shot of your camp with hunters in a natural mood also will add a memorable photo to the scrapbook.

When taking photos of a hunter with a deer, be sure to have both subjects in a natural setting. Avoid a deer laying in the back of a truck or hanging in the garage. You also should wipe the blood away, as it can lead to a tasteless photograph.

Most photographs look better when the hunter is behind the animal. It tends to make the deer appear larger and enlightens the picture. Sometimes, instead of posing and smiling, it is nice to hold the buck by an antler and appear to be looking at it, but be careful not to obscure an impressive rack. Most important, however, is to be sure the sun is at your back. Shooting into the sun will fool your camera and make it believe the area is brighter than it really is. Shadows also should be taken into consideration. Another angle, or a flash may help to remove the shadows. Hunting caps can be raised slightly to remove the shadow over the face.

Different angles will help, along with switching from horizontal to vertical shots. And remember, closeness counts. So many trophy/hunter shots are taken to include the feet of the deer and a large portion of the surrounding brush. A nice head shot with only the upper-half of the hunter will say a lot more for the memory each time you see the picture.

A lot of photographs are missed simply because the photographer was not ready. Anytime you are scouting, make it a point to carry along your equipment. A surprised deer will often stop and give you the opportunity for a quick photo. Be sure your camera is loaded prior to your outing and always be ready.

It is also important to pack along enough film. Sometimes a deer will offer the best photos when you reach the last exposure of your last roll of film.

Film may appear costly, but in all reality it is still inexpensive when you consider the memories. I would not recommend limiting the number of photos to one or two of this and that. When and if a buck approaches, shoot several frames. This increases the chance of having an outstanding photograph. There are far more things one should know to take good photographs than what I have discussed in this chapter. Several books are available from many of the country's leading photographers. I would recommend a lot of reading to anyone who wants to be involved with photography seriously.

Scrapbook photos do not only have to include a hunter with their trophy. The author took this memorable photograph while the hunter tracked a wounded deer.

CHAPTER 14

FARMLAND DEER
IN NORTH AMERICA

Statistics in this chapter may provide you with helpful information for planning a future hunt. Harvests, populations, public hunting areas and food sources are provided if the information was supplied from those who were contacted.

If a state or province failed to respond to the questionnaire, or if they do not have a whitetail hunting season, their listings will not appear.

HUNTING FARMLAND BUCKS

ALABAMA

During the 1991 season, 246,800 Dixieland hunters harvested 294,400 whitetails.

Alabama's deer herd has increased by approximately 1/2 million in the last 10 years. The present deer herd of 1.5 million choose acorns and honeysuckle as their favorite fall\winter food sources. Approximately 26 percent of the state is agricultural.

According to David Nelson of the District Wildlife Office in Demopolis, the best buck area runs along and 20 miles either side of a line from Eufaula in Barbour County, to York in Sumter County. The better public hunting lands are Barbour, Choccolocco and Oakmulgee wildlife management areas.

Nelson says it is Alabama's goal to better manage the resource by controlling deer numbers and improving buck quality.

For more information contact the Alabama Department of Conservation, 64 N. Union St., Montgomery, AL 36130.

ARIZONA

In 1991, the whitetail population was estimated to be 91,000, compared to 54,000 in 1981.

According to Linden Piest of the Game & Fish Department, there is 1,006,316 acres of agricultural land. The best fall and winter food sources are forbs, grasses, acorns and shrubs.

All national forest lands can provide good hunting. Coconino, Yavapai, Greenlee, Navajo and Apache counties have produced the highest buck harvests in recent years.

Piest says the deer in Arizona normally aren't associated with farmland areas. However, deer numbers are increasing after drought-induced weather.

For more information contact the Arizona Game & Fish Department, 2221 W. Greenway Rd., Phoenix AZ 85023-4399.

ARKANSAS

According to Michael Cartwright, Deer/Elk Program Coordinator, the state is developing a statewide management plan that should be implemented in 1992. The major goals are to increase the harvest, reduce depredation problems, increase habitat and deer populations in some areas.

In 1990, approximately 90,000 deer were harvested by 209,518 hunters. This was a 20 percent decrease from the previous year.

An improved oak mast production in the Ozarks in 1990, may have caused bucks to be less concentrated in open type habitat, and less vulnerable to hunters. However, reports indicate the herd has grown steadily each year. The population now stands at 500,000 whitetails.

Counties with the highest buck harvests in 1990 include Union, Dallas, Drew, Cleveland and Ashley. Although 80 percent of the state is considered private land, there are more than 40 wildlife management areas. The highest buck harvests occurred at White Rock, Piney Creeks, Mt. Magazine and Felsenthal WMAs.

For more information contact the Arkansas Game & Fish Commission, #2 Natural Resources Dr., Little Rock AR 72205.

CONNECTICUT

Connecticut deer hunters took a record 9,896 deer during the 1990 season. With the exception of the muzzleloader hunters, all groups experienced increased harvests over 1989. Shotgunners increased an amazing 127 percent.

About 86 percent of the 1990 deer harvests occurred on private land, but controlled hunts are held at Yale Forest, Stone's Ranch and Bristol Water Company.

The total acreage of agricultural land is unknown, but in 1990, 1,653 whitetails were bagged under the class protection program.

For more information contact the Connecticut Department of Environmental Protection, State Office Building, 165 Capital Ave., Hartford, CT 06106.

FLORIDA

The total deer harvest for 1990 was not reported, but the 65 wildlife management areas accounted for almost 6,000 deer.

Ocala Wildlife Management Area led the way in buck harvests with 914, followed by Apalachicola with 349, and Aucilla with 317.

The Wildlife Management Area Forecast for 1991-92 predicted Halfmoon, Aucilla, Tide Swamp, Big Shoals, Arbuckle, Edward Ball and Escambia River to provide excellent hunting.

For more information contact the Florida Game and Fresh Water Fish Commission, Farris Bryant Bldg., 620 S. Meridian St., Tallahassee, FL 32399-1600.

GEORGIA

During the last decade the Georgia whitetail herd has doubled. Hunters during the 1990 season cashed in by bagging more than 200,000 whitetails.

''Traditionally we have had larger populations of deer in the Piedmont area, but now we are seeing an increase in whitetails in the Coastal Plains,'' said Bill Fletcher, Wildlife Biologist.

Fletcher claims about 45 percent of the state is considered agricultural, with a large portion of the farmland in the lower coastal areas. The prime fall/winter food sources are acorns, honeysuckle, corn, soybeans, winter wheat and rye. For more information contact the Georgia Department of Natural Resources, 205 Butler St., S.E., Suite 1362, Atlanta, GA 30334.

INDIANA

Indiana's deer herd doubled from 1982 to 1992, and the 1991 deer harvest was the tenth straight on record.

Hoosier hunters bagged almost 100,000 deer in 1991, compared to 88,763 in 1990. However, the antlered buck harvest of 41,593 was down 3 percent from the previous year.

The south-central portions recorded the highest harvests in 1991, with Brown, Franklin, Kosciusko, Marshall, Noble, Pike, Steuben and Switzerland counties leading the way. The top three buck counties were Kosciusko, Steuben and Switzerland. Although it is not known what percentage of the land is agricultural, the prime fall/winter food sources are corn, soybeans and acorns.

For more information contact the Indiana Department of Natural Resources, Fish and Wildlife Division, 402 W. Washington St., Room W273, Indianapolis, IN 46204.

IOWA

Following the 1991 hunting seasons, officials estimated there were 200,000 deer in Iowa, nearly double the number of 1981.

189

HUNTING FARMLAND BUCKS

The deer kill in 1991 fell to just under 84,000, a decline of about 14 percent from 1990. The counties with the highest harvests were in northeast Iowa in Zone 9, and southeast Iowa in zones 5 and 6. The three counties producing the highest buck harvests were Allamakee, Clayton and Van Buren.

"The best deer habitat occurs where forest mixes with agricultural lands," said Willie Suchy, Wildlife Biologist, explaining that most of these areas are found along Iowa's rivers and larger creeks. "In general, the best deer habitat is in the northeast corner of Iowa and the southern 1/4 of the state."

Approximately 90 percent of Iowa is considered agricultural, either annual crops or hay or pasture. The deer utilize grain from harvested crop fields, and acorns for most of their winter food.

For more information contact the Iowa Department of Natural Resources, Wallace State Office Bldg., Des Moines, IA 50319-0034.

KENTUCKY

The state estimated the deer population in 1992 at 450,000, which was four times higher than it was in 1982.

During the 1990 season, Kentucky hunters bagged 73,920 whitetails, of which 47,661 were bucks. Hopkins County was responsible for the highest buck harvest, but Breckinridge, Christian, Crittenden, Lawrence, Ohio, Owen, Todd and Webster counties followed close behind.

The better public hunting areas include Higginson-Henry and West Kentucky wildlife management areas, Land Between The Lakes and Daniel Boone National Forest.

John Phillips, Deer Program Coordinator, says the state is 40 percent crop and pasture land. The favorable fall/winter food sources are acorns, winter wheat and cover crops.

"Kentucky has placed a large number of deer in the Boone & Crockett records in the past 10 years, and we expect this to increase," Phillips stated.

For more information contact the Department of Fish and Wildlife Resources, #1 Game Farm Rd., Frankfort, KY 40601.

LOUISIANA

The state's deer herd increased by more than 25 percent from 1980 to 1990. The latest population estimate of 650,000 allowed hunters to harvest 194,300 whitetails during the 1990-91 seasons, compared to 105,500 in 1980-81.

The amount of agricultural land was not reported, but according to David Moreland, Deer Study Leader, acorns, winter pastures and winter wheat provide most of the whitetail's fall/winter food supply.

The Northwest and Delta parishes are considered the best in the state for hunting deer. Moreland stated the better public areas are Red River/Three Rivers, Jackson-Bienville wildlife management areas, and the Tensas Wildlife Refuge.

For more information contact the Department of Wildlife and Fisheries, P.O. Box 98000, Baton Rouge, LA 70898-9000.

MAINE

The state has recorded deer harvests for the past 72 years, and the 1990 harvest of 25,977 ranked 34th. The deer herd has increased from 160,000 in 1980 to 230,000 in 1990.

The antlered buck harvest totaled 15,265 in 1980, which represented a 10 percent decline compared to the 1989 harvests. The better buck counties are York, Cumberland and Kennebel.

The Frye Mountain Wildlife Management Area is said to offer good public land hunting. Gerald Lavigne, Wildlife Biologist, reported that only 7 percent of the state is considered agricultural, most of which lies in the central and southern portions.

For more information contact the Maine Division of Fish & Wildlife, P.O. Box 1298, Bangor, ME 04402-1298.

MASSACHUSETTS

Approximately 100,000 hunters bumped heads with the estimated deer herd of 55,000 during the 1991 hunting season.

Gary Vecellio, Deer Project Leader, estimates the herd is growing 6 to 7 percent each year.

Berkshire county usually records the highest harvests of antlered bucks. The public hunting is considered good in both the Mt. Washington and Women's Federation State Forest.

''We do not wish to burden farmers, or any other segment of the human population with too many deer,'' Vecellio said. ''Our management goal is to keep populations at compatible levels.''

For more information contact the Massachusetts Division of Fisheries & Wildlife, One Rabbit Hill Rd., Westboro, MA 01581.

MICHIGAN

Michigan's 1990 deer harvest of 316,400 was the second best on record. However, in the Upper Peninsula the deer harvest fell 13 percent from the previous year.

Prior to the 1991 hunting season, the estimated deer population was 1.6 to 1.75 million. Private land herds have expanded seven times from an estimated 200,000 in 1972.

Many of these deer are in southern Michigan in agricultural or suburban areas.

According to Harry Hill, Wildlife Division Biometrician, there are more than 10 million acres (30 percent) in farmlands. Forest lands comprise another 50 percent. Both corn and soybeans supply the whitetail with an abundance of food in the fall/winter months in the Lower Peninsula.

Ontonagon, Baraga, Iron, Dickinson, Menominee and Schoolcraft counties were responsible for the highest buck harvests in the Upper Peninsula, and Alpena and Iosco in the Lower Peninsula in the 1990 season.

Hill explained the state hopes to increase deer numbers in some areas, and decrease them in others.

"Our goal is to gradually decrease the deer herd to about 1.3 million with a higher proportion of bucks," Hill said.

For more information contact the Michigan Department of Natural Resources, Box 30028, Lansing, MI 48909.

MINNESOTA

Minnesota hunters have steadily increased the deer harvests by a wide margin. In 1991, 220,200 whitetails were harvested, compared to 138,941 in 1984.

Zone 1 led the way in 1991 with a harvest of more than 31,000 bucks, but also had the most participation. The best buck hunting success went to Zone 4 in the central and western portion where hunters enjoyed a 58 percent success. The counties with the highest male harvests were Cass, Itasca, Ottertail and St. Louis.

According to officials, heavy snowfall often causes starvation in the northern areas. In the southern agricultural regions deer have greater access to food plots and waste grains.

For more information contact the Minnesota Department of Natural Resources, 500 Lafayette Rd., St. Paul, MN 55155.

MISSOURI

Missouri reports almost a 50 percent increase in the deer herd from 1981 to 1991. Just prior to the 1990 hunting season, an estimated 800,000 deer roamed the state. Hunters harvested almost half that number.

Statewide, 31 percent is considered forested with the remainder in pasture or agricultural land. The northern part of the state is approximately 12 percent forested, while the Ozarks in the south average 40 to 50 percent forested.

Most of the bigger bucks have come from north of the Missouri River, and Scotland, Harrison, Chariton and Lincoln counties have been responsible for the most entries in Missouri's Big Buck Club Members.

According to Lonnie Hansen, Wildlife Research Biologist, acorns are the most important fall/winter food source, but row crops, alfalfa, clover and winter wheat are utilized heavily where available.

''We feel that deer populations in our farmland areas are reasonably under control,'' said Hansen. ''There will always be hotspots and coldspots that we will have to deal with on an individual basis.''

For more information contact the Missouri Department of Conservation, P.O. Box 180, Jefferson City, MO 65102-0180.

MONTANA

In the 1990 deer season, Montana hunters bagged an estimated 49,419 whitetails, of which 27,000 were antlered bucks.

According to Montana's 1990, 8th Edition of Big Game Trophies, Flathead county has led the way with 11 listings in the Boone & Crockett typical whitetail category. Missoula and Lincoln counties also have ranked high.

In the Pope & Young typical whitetail category there are more than 160 entries. The top counties include Missoula, Flathead, Teton, Powell and Dawson.

For more information contact the Montana Department of Fish, Wildlife and Parks, Wildlife Division, 1420 E. 6th Ave., Helena, MT 59620.

NEBRASKA

Officials estimated the 1991 deer herd to be around 200,000, compared to 125,000 in 1981. Harvests in 1991 exceeded 33,000 for a success rate of almost 50 percent.

Nebraska's Big Game Specialist, Karl Menzel reported that the state is 45 percent agricultural, 50 percent grasslands, and the remaining areas wooded and urban. The basic food sources for the fall/winter months consists of a variety of agricultural crops.

The best counties for bucks are Richardson, Nance, Nemaha, Pawnee, Dakota and Boyd, based on density of harvests. The better public lands include Pine Ridge Division of Nebraska National Forest, Fort Robinson, Bessey Division NNF, and Harlan County Reservoir.

For more information contact the Nebraska Game and Parks Commission, P.O. Box 508, Bassett, NE 68714.

NEW HAMPSHIRE

Bow and gun hunters harvested 8,792 whitetails in 1991 from the estimated herd of 42,000. The highest harvest occurred in Cheshire, Hillsborough and Rockingham counties.

HUNTING FARMLAND BUCKS

State Wildlife Biologist, Scot J. Williamson, claims that 87 percent of New Hampshire is forested, and approximately 6 to 8 percent is agricultural. The best fall/winter foods include acorns, beechnuts, apples and browse.

The White Mountain National Forest is the largest block of public land in the state, and provides most of the public hunting opportunities.

For more information contact the New Hampshire Fish and Game Department, Region 1, Route 3, Box 241, Lancaster, NH 03584.

NEW JERSEY

The 1990 deer harvest of 48,222 was the second largest harvest in the state's records. It represents a 0.7 decrease from the 1989 record harvest of 48,526. The 1990 harvest included 23,141 antlered bucks.

Hunterdon county exceeded the number of deer harvested in any other county. Warren and Sussex counties follow in harvest numbers, and all are located in the northern portion of the state where excessive farming occurs.

The prime food sources for New Jersey's whitetails are corn, soybeans, wheat, oats and rye. According to officials, these crops, as well as strawberries, tomatos, potatoes and orchard-grown fruits supplement the diet of deer in the northern portion of the state.

For more information contact the Division of Fish, Game and Wildlife, 401 E. State St., CN 400, Trenton NJ 08625-0402.

NEW YORK

The 1991 pre-season deer population was estimated at 800,000, compared to 650,000 in 1981.

During the 1990 season, New York hunters harvested 190,810 whitetails. This included more than 103,000 bucks, and was the highest buck harvest in the state's history.

Dutchess and Columbia county in the eastern part of the state, along with Allegany, Steuben, Chemung and Yates counties in the southwest were responsible for the highest buck harvests.

A state farmland study conducted in 1989 showed more than 5 million acres in farmlands, compared to 1.6 million acres of total woodlands. Corn, acorns and other various mast crops provide most of the fall/winter foods.

"New programs allowing hunters to obtain more than one deer management permit and limiting harvest on permits to antlerless deer are being implemented in an effort to improve management," explained Senior Wildlife Biologist, David Riehlman.

For more information contact the New York Department of Environmental Conservation, Game Farm Road, Delmar, NY 12054.

NORTH DAKOTA

The population trend data indicate that the deer herd is high and stable, and surveys show that North Dakota hunters enjoy a high quality hunt.

Hunters bagged more than 43,000 whitetails during the 1990 deer season. Archers enjoyed a 32.8 percent success, while 69.3 percent of the gunners were successful.

The amount of agricultural land was not reported, but whitetails are found throughout the state.

The Department believes that the population has reached optimum levels considering existing habitat and landowner tolerance. By 1995, they hope to maintain the buck-to-doe ratio between one buck to three does, and one buck to seven does.

For more information contact the North Dakota Game and Fish Department, 100 N. Bismarck Expressway, Bismarck, ND 58501-5095.

OHIO

Wildlife Program Administrator, Dave Watts estimated 225,000 to 315,000 whitetails inhabited the state in 1991, compared to 130,000 in 1981. Presently, deer populations are substantially lower in the more intensively farmed western counties and the heavily urbanized northeastern counties.

Of the 98,468 deer harvested during the 1990 season, more than 35,000 were antlered bucks. Counties with the highest harvests include Guernsey, Harrison, Jefferson, Muskingum and Columbiana

According to Watts, the best public hunting is found in Wayne National Forest, located in three different regions of the state.

Although the state is 60 percent agricultural, most of the farmlands are located in western Ohio. Corn and soybeans provide most of the food, while crab, honeysuckle and hay are the prime foods in the eastern portion.

For more information contact the Ohio Department of Natural Resources, Fountain Square, Columbus, OH 43224.

OKLAHOMA

According to Michael Shaw, Research Supervisor, there are 11.5 million acres of agricultural land in the state. In 1992, the estimated whitetail population stood at 275,000, compared to 150,000 in 1982.

The 1990 statistics showed 174,231 bow and gun hunters were afield, increasing the statewide harvest by 118 percent from 1985. Their highest harvests occurred in Osage, Craig, Nowata, Pittsburg and Cherokee counties, with the higher buck harvests in Craig, Pittsburg, Sequoyah and Nowata counties.

Public lands with the highest harvests are Cherokee DHA, Fort Gibson, Gruber and Kaw wildlife management areas.

The prime fall/winter food sources are wheat, clover, honeysuckle, rye and acorns.

"We will be implementing a Deer Management Assistance program in 1992. Landowners with at least 1,000 acres may apply," explained Shaw.

For more information contact the Oklahoma Department of Wildlife Conservation, P.O. Box 53465, Oklahoma City, OK 73152.

PENNSYLVANIA

Deer hunters in the state totaled 1.1 million in 1990, which was also the estimated deer herd in 1991.

During the 1990 season, hunters bagged 415,561 deer, of which 170,101 were antlered bucks. Counties in the northern portion with the highest buck harvests include Bradford, Tioga, Potter, Erie, Warren and Susquehanna. Centre and Clearfield reported the highest buck harvests in the central portion of the state, and Bedford and Somerset in southern Pennsylvania. The counties that produced the highest antlered harvests per square mile of forest were Berks, Columbia, Montour and York.

Approximately 8.2 million acres, or 29 percent of the state's land is agricultural. Clover and corn provide much of the fall/winter food supply in the agricultural areas, while acorns, apples, blueberries, dogwoods and mountain laurel provide most of the food in the forested regions.

William Shope, Supervisor, Forest Wildlife Section, says Pennsylvania has established deer population goals based on forest habitat quality.

For more information contact the Pennsylvania Game Commission, 2001 Elmerton Ave., Harrisburg, PA 17710-9797.

SOUTH DAKOTA

Approximately 225,000 whitetails inhabited the state during the 1990-91 winters, with 1/3 of the herd located in the Black Hills.

Nearly 42,000 whitetails were bagged during the 1990 deer seasons. The projected buck harvest was 23,354. The East River area was responsible for the largest percentage of the buck harvest with 13,661. The Black Hills reported 3,174 bucks harvested. The highest buck harvest by counties went to Brown, Grant, Minnehaha, Codington, Brookings and Turner.

Of the three wildlife refuges, Sand Lake took all honors in 1990 with a harvest of 183 bucks. Approximately 80 percent of the state is agricultural, but 25 percent of that is considered range land, according to Kelly McPhillips of the Resource Analysis Section. Prime fall/winter food sources include waste grain, standing corn and alfalfa stacks.

For more information contact the South Dakota Game, Fish and Parks, 445 East Capitol, Pierre, SD 57501.

TENNESSEE

Although the actual harvest numbers for the 1991 season were not yet known at the time of this writing, officials say approximately 121,000 deer were taken from an estimated population of 700,000. In 1981, hunters bagged 40,000 deer from a population of 275,000.

Counties producing the highest harvests in 1991 include Hardeman, Weakley, Henry, Giles, Hickman and Maury. The best public areas include Fort Campbell, Chuck Swan WMA, Milan AAP, Oak Ridge WMA, Hatchie NWR and Land Between The Lakes.

Greg Wathen, Wildlife Biologist, reports that approximately 50 percent of the state is forested, with the western side being more agricultural. He claims that acorns are the best fall/winter food sources. The 1990 Oak Mast Summary indicated the counties of Benton and Henderson had the best quality ratings of red and white oak.

For more information contact the Tennessee Wildlife Resources Agency, Ellington Agricultural Center, P.O. Box 40747, Nashville, TN 37204.

TEXAS

A recent annual census indicated that Texas had an estimated white-tailed deer herd of 3,537,560. The surveys show a density of 49.5 deer per 1,000 acres. Herd Composition data indicate 21.7 percent are bucks.

In 1990, an estimated 429,532 deer were harvested. The ecological areas with the highest antlered buck harvests in 1990 were Edwards Plateau, South Texas Plains and Pineywoods.

Milo, corn, soybeans and mesquite beans are the preferred fall/winter food sources in the agricultural areas.

For more information contact the Texas Parks And Wildlife Department, 4200 Smith School Rd., Austin, TX 78744.

HUNTING FARMLAND BUCKS

VERMONT

During the 1991 hunting season, hunters bagged 11,584 whitetails. The firearm season accounted for more than 90 percent of the total.

Windsor, Windham, Washington and Rutland counties led the way with the highest number of bucks harvested per square mile.

According to the Agency of Natural Resources, the deer hunting is best in the northeastern corner of the state. Much of this area is blessed with abandoned apple orchards and fields. The agency also reported that the biggest bucks are generally found in the higher elevations.

For more information contact the Vermont Agency of Natural Resources, 103 South Main St., 10 South, Waterbury, VT 05676.

VIRGINIA

More than 300,000 hunters harvested 204,906 deer during the 1991-92 season.

Virginia's 1991 deer herd was estimated at 850,000 compared to 480,000 animals in 1981.

Bedford, Loudon, Southhampton, Bath and Pittsylvania counties were responsible for the highest harvests in the 1991-92 season.

Approximately 30 percent of the state is agricultural, with a higher proportion in Northern Piedmont, Shenandoah Valley and Coastal Plain. The best fall/winter food sources are acorns and honeysuckle.

''Virginia's deer herd is large and continues to grow,'' said Patrick D. Keeper, District Wildlife Biologist. ''The Deer Management Assistance Program allows for quality deer management while Deer Crop Assistance Program allows for additional harvests to relieve excessive crop damage.''

For more information contact the Department of Game and Inland Fisheries, 4010 West Broad St., Box 11104, Richmond, VA 23230.

WEST VIRGINIA

An estimated 400,000 archery and firearm hunters bagged more than 175,000 whitetails during the 1991 seasons.

Officials say about 800,000 deer roamed the state in 1991, compared to 500,000 in 1981. The highest deer populations occur in the northern portion.

The top five counties in buck harvests were Randolph, Ritchie, Preston, Hampshire and Lewis. The best public hunting include the Little River, Blackwater and Potomac wildlife management areas.

Approximately 20 percent of the state is agricultural land, with acorns, beechnuts, black cherries and various browse providing most of the fall/winter foods.

According to Jack Cromer, Supervisor of Game Management Services, the deer populations are gradually reaching recommended levels.

For more information contact the West Virginia Division of Natural Resources, Operation Center, P.O. Box 67, Elkins, WV 26241.

WISCONSIN

Approximately 1.35 million whitetails roamed the state just prior to the 1991 hunting seasons. However, after the harvests of more than 424,000, the overwinter population stood at 925,000.

HUNTING FARMLAND BUCKS

Wisconsin has several thousand acres open to public hunting in the form of county, state and federal forests. The highest buck harvests in 1990 occurred in the Western district, but was only slightly higher than the Lake Michigan and North Central districts.

William Ishmael, Deer, Bear and Furbearer Ecologist, reported that approximately 12,506,900 acres of farmland produced crops in 1990. About 80 to 85 percent of the crops are located in the southern part of the state. Alfalfa, corn, soybeans and various other grains provide much of the food in the fall/winter months.

According to Ishmael, the deer herd is at an all-time high, and crop damage has reached record levels.

''Deer damage permits are one of the methods that we use to help eliminate the problems. However, they are used as one alternative to help solve some immediate damage, and not meant to decrease the statewide population,'' explained Ishmael. Ishmael also says the future of Wisconsin's deer seasons are bright, and that hunters have more opportunities to harvest deer than ever before.

For more information contact the Wisconsin Department of Natural Resources, Box 7921, Madison, WI 53707.

WYOMING

At least 45 percent of the state is considered agricultural, with alfalfa, winter wheat and range land providing most of the fall/winter foods.

In 1990, the whitetail herd was estimated at 54,031. A little more than 20,000 rifle hunters bagged 9,388 deer, while enjoying a 45 percent success. Only 1,080 bowhunters pursued whitetails, and 147 deer were bagged.

Crook, Johnson and Campbell counties, along with the Black Hills and Powder River areas provided the best hunting. However, a large portion of these are privately owned. The better public ground are hunt areas 2 and 4 of the Black Hills, according to officials.

Daryl Lutz, Wildlife Biologist, says the whitetail population is increasing on private lands. "Typically, we are forced with paying depredation claims from damage by deer on cash crops," Lutz said.

For more information contact the Wyoming Game and Fish Department, 5400 Bishop Blvd., Cheyenne, WY 82006.

PROVINCES OF CANADA

ALBERTA

Approximately 165,000 whitetails inhabited the province as of 1991, compared to 120,000 in 1985. In 1990, hunters cashed in on 26,596 whitetails, of which 20,191 were bucks. Region 4, located in southeast Alberta, reported the highest harvest of bucks, followed by Region 5 in the east-central portion.

About 35 percent of the province is considered agricultural land. The main fall and winter food sources include snowberry, silverberry, chokecherry, rose, aspen, aster and alfalfa.

According to William Glasgow, Wildlife Management Biologist, populations increased during the last decade due to milder than average winters.

For more information contact the Alberta Forestry, Lands And Wildlife, Petroleum Plaza, North Tower, 9945-108 St., Edmonton, Alberta T5K 2G6.

HUNTING FARMLAND BUCKS

MANITOBA

Hunters harvested more than 30,000 whitetails during the 1991 season in Manitoba. The estimated population stood at 125,000, compared to 100,000 in 1981.

According to Ronald Larche, Provincial Deer Biologist, 70 percent of Manitoba's deer range is predominantly farmland. The preferred fall/winter food sources include corn, sunflower, acorns, fall rye, alfalfa, snowberry and silverberry.

The hunting areas reporting the highest harvests are the agricultural portions of Manitoba, specifically the southwestern and south Interlake regions.

''Manitoba's deer population is currently high due to a series of mild winters,'' said Larche.

For more information contact the Manitoba Natural Resources, Wildlife Branch, Box 24, 1495 St. James St., Winnipeg, Manitoba R3H 0W9.

NOVA SCOTIA

During the 1990 hunting season more than 80,000 hunters bagged 16,166 whitetails. Counties with the highest harvests were Lunenburg, Hants, Halifax, Colchester and Inverness. Of the total harvest 9,396 were bucks.

Approximately 10 percent of the province is in agricultural production. Deer habitat accounts for about 80 percent of the remainder. The best fall/winter foods are hardwood browse near the farming edges, woodlots and the smaller cut-over blocks that offer regrowth.

In 1992 the deer herd was estimated to be 90,000, and was about 13,000 less than in 1982. According to Tony Nette and Morton Stewart of the Wildlife Resources Division, the decline is due to the herd having exceeded the carrying capacity of the range.

"The herd is now in good shape and numbers appear to be increasing," said Nette.

For more information contact the Nova Scotia Department of Natural Resources, Wildlife Division, 136 Exhibition St., Kentville, Nova Scotia B4N 4E5.

QUEBEC

In 1990 the reported harvest for Quebec was 21,059 on the mainland, and 7,304 on Anticosti Island.

According to Gilles Lamontagne, Big Game Biologist, the 1992 deer population on the mainland stands around 175,000, compared to 85,000 in 1982. The estimated herd on Anticosti Island is believed to be about 120,000, the same as it was in 1982.

Only 1 percent of Anticosti Island is agricultural. However, farmland constitutes some mainland, with the highest percentage in zones 4 through 9, located in the southcentral part of the province.

Lamontagne says the best zone for deer hunting is Anticosti Island, but it is only accessible by an outfitter organization.

For more information contact the Department of Recreation, Fish And Game, Place dela Capitale 150 East, St-Cyrille Blvd., Quebec City, Quebec G1R 4Y1.

SASKATCHEWAN

High hunter participation and good hunting conditions have contributed to a deer harvest increase of 21 percent from 29,399 deer in 1987, to 35,470 deer in 1988. The 1992 deer herd was estimated at 200,000 to 250,000—roughly the same as the 1982 estimate.

HUNTING FARMLAND BUCKS

The Parkland ecozone supports the highest deer densities, and accounted for the highest proportion of the harvest.

According to Dave Brewster, Province Deer Specialist, the southeast and north-central areas produce a large percentage of the antlered bucks.

Brewster says the province has a damage prevention program to help control crop damage.

"We have to provide more liberal hunting opportunities, and increased seasons for non-residents, lifetime licenses for residents, and either sex hunts," Brewster said.

For more information contact the Saskatchewan Parks and Renewable Resources, 3211 Albert St., Regina, Saskatchewan S4S 5W6.

CHAPTER 15

THE DAYS TO COME

Any deer hunter would find it hard to believe that the survival of the white-tailed deer could ever be in jeopardy. They have adapted to our busy world and are expanding within the city limits of many large metropolitan areas.

But the deer hunter must be concerned with the future of pursuing these crafty animals. Many things have already affected that outlook, and it appears that more will follow. Our world has become civilized, perhaps over-civilized, and we, the deer hunter, are no longer a pioneer of the land. The deer hunter, regardless of their woodsmanship abilities, appears as a blood-thirsty, ruthless character to many. More about that in a moment. First, I'd like to say a few things about habitat.

To put it bluntly, we have become infected with suburbanization in recent decades. Every day of the week, in nearly every area of North America, some form of construction occurs. Now don't get me wrong; I know we must expand. I am as guilty as those I am about to discuss, since I am a country boy with a house sitting close to a deer woods. But I believe our wildlife could someday run out of places to hide if we are not careful.

It begins when the construction of a business or home occurs close to the city. Later, another dwelling appears a little further from the last. Before you know it, these residential or commercial districts become part of the city. The countryside soon becomes a cycle of expansion that can't stop until it bumps into another.

I sincerely feel this growing concern will need changing if we expect to see our wildlife (includes farmland deer) flourish. I don't have the answers, but I do believe a solution will someday be needed.

The loss of habitat has already affected several species of wildlife. I can remember flushing ten rabbits in one hour of walking. But that was twenty years ago. It was also before several new roads and building projects destroyed escape cover that the cottontail depended on for survival.

As long as the whitetail has cover, whether it be the neighbor's 2-acre maple woods, or farmer Jones' cornfield, the deer will survive. But will there be land to hunt? The more our land is broken into smaller parcels, the less opportunity we will have.

Roads, which are necessary for the industrious world we live in, have also led to the destruction of valuable wildlife habitat, not to mention the devastation of vehicles and lives from deer/vehicle collisions, or the big dollars that insurance companies pay because of damages resulting from these collisions. However, our countrysides, according to some, need more roads. As for me, I would just as soon cover a few extra miles, and if necessary, use the roads we now have, or see my tax dollars repair a few of the aged potholes.

Thus far, the whitetail has adapted to man's busy world. The increase of suburbanization in many areas will test the deer's ability to continue.

Frankly, we do have too many whitetails in many states. If you looked at a particular state or province in the preceding chapter, you may have read about the problems several of our wildlife divisions face. They must reduce the herd to lower numbers, yet keep everybody happy. Seems like they increase the number of extra tags, and a few hunters protest their decision. I believe, though, we must back our game and fish departments whether we agree or not with their conclusion.

Perhaps I have gotten the point across that we do have enough deer. But it won't help me or you if there aren't any areas to hunt. The amount of public lands have decreased in some states, and others have become over-crowded. The private lands continue to break up every time a large parcel is broken into smaller pieces of properties. And as long as we continue expanding, it will continue to happen.

Logging has increased considerably in recent years. I have seen several hundred acres of timber and beautiful land flattened and destroyed in just a few months. I am not against logging, however. It is necessary in our environment, and many deer capitalize after it occurs. The clearcuts become a valuable food source and also provide cover when the undergrowth begins to mature.

Although I have enjoyed many successful hunts in these areas, I do feel that logging is sometimes overdone. If regulations could protect particular portions of land in a given area, while allowing other shares to be cut, the deer would benefit, and so would our countrysides. This would reduce the number of roads that open to poachers, and protect vast areas from being cleaned over a short period of time.

I would estimate that 60 to 80 percent of our deer herds live on private lands in most states. Many farmers have certainly done an excellent job of supplying both food and cover, the two necessary ingredients for a hearty whitetail herd. And when forest cutting occurs in areas where needed, an ample supply of new growth will keep the herd healthy, providing escapes are also available. Landowners must establish effective plans that include these ingredients if they hope to keep deer in the area. A properly managed herd will need both nutrition and cover to guarantee a high rate of reproduction.

The trophy buck has become a highlight in recent years. These tricky rascals are learning our ways and avoiding us hands down. But our potential of taking a crafty, mature buck may soon decrease if bag limits do not focus on antlerless deer whenever necessary.

One example includes the shooting of velvet bucks in the late summer months. Although I just mentioned the need to back our state's wildlife decisions, this is one I find hard to swallow. Some states allow this practice to occur in July and August. Tags are given to landowners that report substantial crop damage.

This routine will reduce the herd by one each time a buck is harvested. But if a doe is harvested, it may reduce the number by three when the crops begin the following spring. I have witnessed a few deer hunters that take advantage of the deer control tags. They go into the fields with the necessary tags and

Deer/vehicle collisions have caused major problems for state wildlife officials and insurance companies.

make it a point to hunt antlered bucks only. They pass the does intentionally, hoping to cash in on a wall-hanger. And many do it very easily, simply because summer bucks are prone to feed in the open fields in daylight hours. If a landowner can shoot ten deer for compensation of crop damage, then why not allow only antlerless deer. Killing the does will do a far better job of controlling the herd, and the bucks would still be around when the hunting season begins.

I enjoy shooting bucks, but I really like getting a big deer. Most other deer hunters feel the same. We shoot enough 1 1/2-year-olds during the hunting season. Why make it any more difficult by harvesting bucks out of the hunting season. In addition, we lose many antlered deer to poachers. They really get a kick out of stealing our deer, which also limits the number of mature bucks.

Enough said about that. The anti's are another problem we must deal with to protect the future of all hunting. They have tried for decades to persuade the courts to stop hunting, and they probably will continue this practice for years to come.

Perhaps you are familiar with *Proposition 200*. At the time of this writing it had just been defeated. Prop 200 was started by various organizations and individuals to stop hunting and fishing in Arizona. When it finally came down to a decision, it was the voters who decided that Prop 200 was not in the best interest of the wildlife or people of Arizona.

I've never been against voting. It's usually the diplomatic way of deciding what is sometimes best. I added *sometimes* because it doesn't necessarily mean that a vote will determine what's best.

In the case of Prop 200, had the majority voted the other way, it could have stopped hunting for all species in the entire state. That would not have been best, but it could have happened.

214

The author photographed this sign along a South Dakota highway.

I have one major problem dealing with votes that could affect the future of all hunting. How does it get into the hands of the people, and why should they decide the outcome when it requires some education in wildlife management?

This certainly is not the people's fault. They can't help it when the courts decide that they should vote on whether hunting should be abolished. The courts should see fit to turn this over to our qualified wildlife experts.

Wildlife biologists spend a few years in college preparing for the job of managing wildlife. And it appears they all agree that hunting is the most effective tool for managing our wildlife. Some courts, however, will often decide it is best to let the uneducated public decide how wildlife should be controlled. Such was the case of Prop 200. The people of Arizona, bluntly speaking, took the task of deciding who would be managing the wildlife. Thank goodness, they put the job back into the hands of the proper authorities.

Actually, the anti's are in the wrong, and it seems a shame we can't take them to court. It is perfectly legal to hunt when regulations are followed. And it's not a crime for them to protest our methods, so long as they do not cause interference. But when they make us out to be barbaric, blood- thirsty slobs (as one individual put it) to the non-hunting public, we should have a right to challenge their accusations. After all, people are sued every day of the week for slander. Actually, there is a **Hunter Harassment Law.** It is prohibited for any individual to harass or distract a wild animal or fish in a way that prevents its harvest; obstruct a person engaged in an activity associated with lawful hunting or fishing; disturbing the property of someone engaged in lawful hunting or fishing; disturbing a lawfully placed hunting blind. Penalties for these violations will vary.

If the anti's really want to do something productive for wildlife, why don't they spend their money wisely. They have spent thousands of dollars in courts attempting to stop hunting. If they used that money to aid in habitat preservation, where needed, and to curtail poaching, the wildlife would surely benefit.

Though this has sounded quite discouraging, there is good news. Hunting and fishing organizations have supported us by contributing a great deal of money to fight the anti-hunting movement. Fortunately, we have won several court battles.

Dealing with the anti's is another matter. When confronted and challenged by an animal activist group, it becomes easy to lose control. However, this often makes the hunter appear as the instigator. It also can lead to added publicity in their favor.

It is best to ignore them and go on about your business. If they attempt to obstruct your hunting privilege, authorities should be contacted to handle the matter.

Youngsters need to be introduced to the outdoors. The future of hunting may depend on their participation.

We should keep in mind, another group of people called *non-hunters* are found throughout our society. These people do not stand against hunting. They simply choose not to partici- pate. I believe, though, we must win their vote. To do this we must not use the term *sport hunting*. This can quickly turn a non- hunter into an anti. While many of us do hunt for sport, it should also be emphasized that the meat is a desired aspect of the hunt.

A few weeks prior to preparing this chapter, I came across a bowhunting magazine dated 1978. Three pages into the publication I came across an editorial that discussed the anti- hunting problems. Apparently, even though I did not take it seriously at that time, the issue was already building steam.

I have been ridiculed by an anti-hunter for eating meat. Now I don't know about you, but I really like the stuff when it's cooked well. That applies to beef, pork, birds of various types, venison and a few others. But this person made it sound like eating meat was an evil thing. We all have this choice, and I do not criticize anyone for not wanting to eat meat. However, I don't believe the anti's should use this against us. As I told the lady who shamed me, "My ancestors ate meat; I'm going to eat it and so are my children."

For some strange reason, the anti's normally put animals above people. I sincerely believe they have forgotten that the human race is the superior being. We should rule over the animals regardless of how civilized this world has become.

They also do their share of misplacing the predator. I have explained this to a few that have failed to understand that man is a predator, just like the coyote who stalks a rabbit, or the mountain lion that stalks a deer. Man, the superior predator, needs to stalk. Most of us are somewhat determined to hunt and pursue. Maybe it's nothing more than a carry-over from our ancestors. We no longer must hunt for survival, but the need remains. Unlike the anti's that have not experienced this great satisfaction, we have been there. And we have learned, the gratification goes much further than a kill.

Youngsters will play a major role in tomorrow's hunting. We must continue to introduce kids into an ethical, pleasurable world of hunting. Simply said, we cannot afford to run out of manpower.

The U.S. Fish and Wildlife Service introduced a report in 1992 that showed a decline in the number of those who hunted in 1991 compared to 1990. The drop of 86,000 was somewhat minor, considering more than 15.5 million hunted. But any reduction, regardless of how much, lowers the manpower needed to fight against those who want to abolish hunting in our civilized world.

We will continue to defeat our own message if we do not stick together. I have heard gunners and bowhunters squabble about the ethics of equipment. What difference does it make if we shoot a compound or longbow, or a primitive or sophisticated muzzleloader? As long as it is used legally, it should be each hunter's choice.

I will never lose my compelling desire to hunt. They can take away the land, and they can take away my gun and bow, but they can't take away my obsessive needs. Without it, I would be incomplete.

HUNTING FARMLAND BUCKS

Farmland deer have thrived in North America during the last decade.   Hunting and fishing organizations on the national, state and local levels, game and fish departments, sportsmen and conservationists have made this possible.

INDEX